Studies In The Book Of Hebrews

By
E.J.Waggoner

Given at the 32nd Session of the
General Conference in 1897

TEACH Services, Inc.
www.TEACHServices.com

World rights reserved. This book or any portion thereof may not be copied or reproduced in any form or manner whatever, except as provided by law, without the written permission of the publisher, except by a reviewer who may quote brief passages in a review.

The author assumes full responsibility for the accuracy of all facts and quotations as cited in this book. The opinions expressed in this book are the author's personal views and interpretation of the Bible and do not necessarily reflect those of TEACH Services, Inc.

Copyright © 1998,2003 TEACH Services, Inc.
ISBN-13: 978-1-57258-021-3
Library of Congress Control Number: 94-61581

Published by
TEACH Services, Inc.
www.TEACHServices.com

Table of Contents

Study Number One 1
(Tuesday Afternoon, February 9, 1897)
Study Number Two 9
(Wednesday Afternoon, February 10, 1897)
Study Number Three 15
(Thursday Afternoon, February 11, 1897)
Study Number Four 21
(Friday Afternoon, February 12, 1897)
Study Number Five 27
(Sunday Afternoon, February 14, 1897)
Study Number Six 33
(Monday Afternoon, February 15, 1897)
Study Number Seven 41
(Tuesday Afternoon, February 16, 1897)
Study Number Eight 51
(Wednesday Afternoon, February 17, 1897)
Study Number Nine 61
(Thursday Afternoon, February 18, 1897)
Study Number Ten 71
(Sunday Afternoon, February 28, 1897)
Study Number Eleven 77
(Monday Afternoon, February 22, 1897)
Study Number Twelve 85
(Tuesday Afternoon, February 23, 1897)
Study Number Thirteen 95
(Wednesday Afternoon, February 24, 1897)
Study Number Fourteen 99
(Thursday Afternoon, February 25, 1897)
Study Number Fifteen 109
(Friday Afternoon, February 26, 1897)
Study Number Sixteen 119
(Sunday Afternoon, February 28, 1897)
Study Number Seventeen 131
(Monday Afternoon, March 1, 1897)
Study Number Eighteen 139
(Tuesday Afternoon, March 2, 1897)

Study Number One
(Tuesday Afternoon, February 9, 1897)

"According to the announcement, and my wish as well, this is to be a Bible study. But in order that we really may have a Bible class, we must have some who will do Bible study. Now, I know that the circumstances here are most unfavorable for Bible study. We cannot have a Bible school here as we would if we had come together for that purpose alone, because the day is quite largely filled with other meetings; and, aside from meetings, there are many here who have other duties to perform, so that the time for actual study is very limited. Yet I think we may, any of us, find one hour each day for Bible study. We should find that much time at least each morning to devote to this purpose. Open your Bibles, if you please, to the book of Hebrews. Let some one begin to read, and, without any break, let somebody else follow, taking verse by verse in this first chapter of Hebrews, each one looking upon his Bible during the reading."

(The chapter is now read.)

"First, let us take this up verse by verse, and notice what it says, each statement,—and notice what it says, each word; and recognize what it says.

"What is the subject of this chapter?"

"Christ."

"Who is the One first spoken of here?"

"God."

"God is the one, then, first spoken of. That is the first thing we know, because when we stand at the beginning of the chapter, supposedly we do not know what follows. The first thing we meet in this book is what?"

"God."

"That is the beginning. What about God? What has he done?"

"He spoke."

"God spoke. When?"

"In times past."

"To whom did he speak?"

"To the fathers."

"How did he speak?"

"By the prophets."

"He has spoken—how often?"

"Many times. Sundry times."

"Yes, God spoke. What does he still do?"

"He speaks. He still speaks."

"He speaks; he hath spoken. To what time does that expression, `He hath spoken,' refer?"

"To the past."

"It is completed action. `He hath spoken.' Of course, but to what time does it bring that completed action?"

"To the present."

"To whom has he spoken?"

"To us."

"To whom does he speak?"

"To us; to me."

"Very well; there isn't anything in this world that all men, including you and me, need to know and understand and appreciate more than this simple thing. We have God in this. I know in my own experience, when I just stop still from everything, and think of that, it works wonders. Now what have we learned so far in this lesson?"

"God speaks to me."

"God speaks. God *speaks*. If we didn't know anything more about the Bible than that, there would be a great deal in that. Whatever other portions of the Bible have by previous study become familiar, we can, of course, let fall into place as we study here the nature of the Word, the living Word. That fact that God speaks—is it always kept in mind? Do we always act as though he were speaking? God *has* spoken and he *does* speak. To whom does he speak?"

"To us."

"How does he speak to us?"

"By his Son."

"Has any one present a different rendering of that, a different reading?"

(One with the Greek original) "In his Son."

"Yes, I think the Revised Version gives the same; and that is exactly the literal in that case. What is the reason that the precepts, the promises—the precepts are the promises—of the Bible do not have more effect upon us,—do not take hold of us more than they do?—We don't recognize God as speaking. It is unbelief. We can't see the force of the point. People think they believe the Bible if they believe that God at one time, a long while ago, said something. But they may believe all that, so far as that goes, and not believe the Bible at all for any good to them. The idea unconsciously obtains in the minds of some of those people, that the Word has grown old,—that it was spoken so long ago that the life has dried up in it, and so the Word comes to us as a shell. It doesn't come to us as a shell, but we take it as such. Then what is the living thing that is presented to us here for our present faith to lay hold upon?"

"God speaks."

"What is the nature of the Word of God?"

"Power. Spirit. Life. John 6:63."

"The Word is Spirit, and it is life, for God himself is life. The Word of the living God liveth and abideth forever. Eternal Word!

"Now, what is the characteristic of that which is eternal,—the characteristic of God, of Christ, of heaven, and of the earth when it is made new to abide forever?"

"Immortal, unchanging, living."

"Does God grow old?"

"No."

"How much older is God to–day than he was in the beginning?"

"Not any."

"What is his name?"

"I AM."

"I AM. I *AM*. Then he isn't any older than he was a million years ago. How much older, then, is his Word, that was spoken to the fathers by the prophets? No older, is it? How old is it?"

"Everlasting."

"Why, it is just now as though he were speaking to–day to us. We have this additional statement: He hath spoken to us by his Son. But calling on your knowledge of the Bible, how did he speak to the fathers?"

"Through the prophets."

"But how did he speak to them by the prophets?"

"In his Son."

"What spirit was in the prophets when they spoke?"

"The spirit of Christ."

"Then we might read it in this way: God, who in times past spoke unto the fathers through the prophets, hath in these last days spoken to us in his Son, in whom yet he continues to speak all the time; and that Word which he spoke so long ago (as it seems to us), and which is so old as we reckon time, is just as fresh and living as ever. Last year, when I was crossing the North Sea, I fell in with a man who was a very pleasant companion, but an infidel. We talked a great deal, and he asked me, `How do you know the Bible is true?' He didn't believe that it was true at all. He didn't believe anything in it. I said, `My friend, how do you know I am talking to you? How do you know?' He said, `Why, I hear you.' `You hear; you know. Could you absolutely know in any other way that I am talking to you, if you did not hear me speaking?' Well, this is the only way we can know that this is God's Word—by hearing him speak to us. Now I know that this is God's Word, because he speaks to me, and I hear him; and when we come to that truth, there is no chance for any quibble or equivocation. You do not think of raising the question while I am at present speaking, Now perhaps it is not you that is speaking; perhaps it is somebody else. There is no room for that question, is there? You know I am speaking, because you hear me; and we know God because he speaks. If we do not know that, how can we believe? Did not Christ say that the Jews knew him not, because they could not hear him? Yet was not that Word spoken for the purpose of causing them to believe in Christ? He said, `This voice came not because of me, but for your sakes.' Did those get out of it what they might? Yet did they not hear the voice? Now, is this not the way that a good many read the Bible? It is a voice, an expression. You read the words and get the sound, but you have not come to the place where you hear the voice of God. There is something else besides the voice of God which you want to hear—you want to hear the Word itself. I do not know of anything in the world that has helped me more than to stop and hear God speak. I may say, God, speak; and then listen, and he speaks; and then take up the Bible and read, and thus hear God speaking. The Word of God; he speaks to the fathers by the prophets in the Son in these last days,—`in the last of these days,' literally,—speaks to us in the Son; he is speaking. When God spoke on Sinai, Moses spoke in answer to the voice; and then when God spoke the ten words, what does the Bible say the people did?"

"They trembled. They besought that the Word should not be spoken to them any more."

"Yes, that was a bad thing. They would rather have a man talk to them than God. What is God? Is he not life? What is the nature of his Word? If they had received God's words as living words, they would not have entreated Moses that the voice discontinue. No; they heard the Word just the same as we often hear it, and did not recognize it as the living Word of God speaking to them; hence they were afraid. They feared it would kill them. God would not speak to his children in such a manner that his words would destroy them. Let us read Ex.20:18–21: `And all the people saw the thunderings, and the lightnings, and the noise of the trumpet, and the mountain smoking: and when the people saw it, they removed, and stood afar off. And they said unto Moses, Speak thou with us, and we will hear: but let not God speak with us, lest we die. And Moses said unto the people, Fear not: for God is come to prove you, and that his fear may be before your faces, that ye sin not. And the people stood afar off, and Moses drew near unto the thick darkness where God was.' What was the characteristic of Moses?"

"Meekness; timidity."

"Yet there is another qualification which goes with that, and this is mentioned in the book of Hebrews. He was faithful. He was not afraid to draw near, or that he would die as a result of his approaching God. He drew near to the mount that quaked and smoked, burned and thundered. And what was the thundering?"

"The voice of God."

Now, there is coming a time when that voice will be heard again, and the trump, too. Some will be afraid, frightened, and will seek hiding-places. Others will say, Lo, this is our God; we will be joyful, we will be glad. Why?—Because they have learned to know the sound of the trump. They know that when God speaks, it is life. It is life, and it doesn't make any difference in what form he speaks; it is life, and they know it, and are not at all afraid. If he whispers, all right; if he thunders, well. At that time the trump waxes louder and louder, and we will not run to get from the voice; we will know it.

(One reading the Greek original) "God thundereth marvelously with his voice."

"Yes; God doeth marvelous things. Now I have known people, and I myself am one of them, who have at times come into places where the Word of God was spoken, and where one was present whom I knew or felt sure had the Word of the Lord to speak, a message from the Spirit of God, and yet I have been afraid. It is supposed that all present believe in the Spirit of Prophecy,—God speaking through a person still to his people; but I have known people to be afraid that they have received a testimony from the Lord. Doubtless some of you have had experience in this. I have known people who, when a testimony was read, lost all heart and hope and courage, and became despondent and downhearted. What was the trouble? Was it not that they did not know the voice of God,—that they had not yet learned the joyful sound? Yet, if a person will not be in a proper condition of mind to hear the voice of God, what will he do when he hears the voice? Will he not stand afar off? In this time which is coming, will it be a good thing to stand afar off? No, we want to draw near at that time. Will not only those who know the voice of the Lord want to draw near at that time? How many ways has God of speaking? Many? Then we want to get acquainted with the different phases of God's voice. It is not enough to know just one sound, for if he speaks in many ways, we must be able to recognize all in order to be able to recognize God at all times when he speaks to us. This thought of knowing the voice of God in all its forms will perhaps come to us as we continue the study of the book of Hebrews. No one hath seen the Father. Christ is the shining out and glory; and when the glory shines forth from Christ, it is the shining out of the glory of God. Still further: He is the express image of the Father. Express image; now what word do we use quite commonly which might be a synonym of this, and which, although we hardly ever remember the fact, comes direct from the Greek?—The word character. What is the idea of character—what is the character of man? Is it not just what he is? Well, this is the word used here.

"Whom hath he appointed heir of all things?—Christ. Notice the next phrase, `being the brightness of his glory, and the express image of his person.' Also, `upholding all things by the word of his power.' He himself is the Word. He upholds all things by his powerful Word. Again, `when he had by himself purged our sins.' Purging our sins—what synonym does it suggest to your minds?"

"Rinse. Cleanse. Wash."

Now let us read the third verse in the light of what we have learned this afternoon: Who, because he is the shining of his glory, and the very imprinted character of his substance, and upholds all things by the word of his power, by himself purged our sins, and sat down on the right hand of the Majesty on high.

"Now, does that convey a more striking thought to you than before? He himself purged our sins because he is the Son of the Father; because he is the brightness, because he is the character of his Father; because he upholds all things. Now take that word `uphold.' Can you give an equivalent?"

"Holds up. Carries. Bears."

"Yes, bears or maintains, carries. `Bears' is exactly the first definition of the word which is given there in the text in the Greek. Bears all things; that makes it more forcible to my mind. What is Christ?"

"The express image of God's person."

"What does he do?"

"He bears all things by the Word."

"He bears all things by the Word, or by himself. Because he does all that, what can he do?"

"Cleanse us from sin."

"This thing that is about to be sin in us; suppose we let him bear it, and let him bear us; then what will it be?"

"Righteousness to us."

"See? Because he himself bears all things, therefore by himself he purges us all of sin."

"Our time has expired. Now let our theme for study tomorrow afternoon be this first chapter, verse by verse, as we have begun. Question it; it is all right. If I should speak to you, and you do not understand, you say, `Please repeat that sentence.' There is no other way in which you can find out. It is all right to question the Lord in like manner; and remember, we can come face to face with the Lord, and question him, and that is the only way we can hear him speak. Speak to him in his Word; talk to him; ask what he says, and get him to repeat that over and over again, until it becomes an unmistakable message to yourself. Study every expression that he uses, and then you will be able to look into it, and see the force of it."

Study Number Two
(Wednesday Afternoon, February 10, 1897)

Let us remember that we cannot know anything except as we find it in the Word. I am not here to unload something upon you, to tell you something that I have studied out or found out in any way; but we are here together, both you and I, to study the Word and see what the Lord has said to us; and to see that God speaks to every one of us, and not to a few special ones, and that we may all learn to understand him when he speaks.

As we stand at the beginning of this chapter, we stand face to face with God, who speaks to us through his Son. It is no new thing for God to speak, for he spake in times past to the fathers and prophets, and he now speaks unto us by Christ. It seems to me that the book of Hebrews represents in a striking way what we find in the whole Bible. It starts out with God, and in the whole Bible we stand face to face with God. Here we may pause with reverence. God in these last days has spoken to us by his Son. He spake once and still he speaks to us through his Word. First, God spoke and created, which in the Psalms is expressed, "He spake, and it was." He created all things in Christ, because he is the Word, and God spake in him; therefore all things are created in him. And further, we learn that Christ is the brightness of God's glory, the shining forth of his glory. There is no difference between the Father and the Son. The Son is the express character of God's being.

Question.—If there is no difference between the Father and the Son, how could Christ say, "The Father is greater than I am"?

I don't know. Now you will pardon me if I dwell for a moment upon this question without personal reference to anybody. What conditions make it possible for us to hear in general whoever may speak? If we do not hear, what conditions prevent our hearing? Sometimes a person may not speak loud enough or distinctly enough. Is it possible for those conditions to obtain when God is speaking?—No. Does not God speak distinctly enough to be heard, and clearly enough to be understood, and loud enough to be heard?—Most certainly. Then if the fault is not with him, and we do not hear, what is the trouble?—We do not listen. Now, suppose I were here to talk this afternoon, and I should begin to talk, and each one of you should at the same time begin to talk to his neighbor, you would not be able to hear much of what I said. And if there was one here who did not say anything, but was trying to listen, the talking of the others would make it difficult for him to hear. Now, my experience and observation has been, and doubtless yours has been so, that one reason why we do not hear when the Lord speaks is that we do not give him a chance to speak; we break in on him. He begins to speak, and before he has time to finish the sentence we begin to talk back to him, or we straightway forget that he is talking, and begin with our neighbors, and say, I don't know how that can be. What do you think about that anyhow? We would not treat a brother that way, because it is not polite. Now, does not God have a right to be heard, at least until he is done speaking, before we begin to answer back? You all agree that he has that right. It is fair that God should have a chance to finish what he is saying before we begin to answer back.

You told me something about the nature of God's Word; it liveth and abideth forever. God in times past spake; has he finished speaking?—No. Then it is not yet time for us to talk. He is talking yet. What does he say in the Psalms?—"Be still, and know that I am God." Brethren, the only way we can learn is by keeping still. I do not mean to say that we should not ask questions; that is all right, but hold to just what God says, and do not doubt one thing that God says plainly because he says something else we do not understand. Because God says something in one place we cannot understand, we often doubt something that we can understand. That is not right. Hold to what he says, and you will find out in time that which you do not understand.

Now return to the thought in the chapter: Christ stands as the brightness of God's glory and the express image of his person,—just the very impress and the shining forth of the glory of God. Christ is the Word, and the Word which he speaks is spirit and life. When he speaks that Word which is spirit and life, he speaks his own life. So when we read, He bears all things by the word of his power, we see in that not that only, but we see in that that he bears all things himself. So he speaks, he creates, he bears, he has purged our sins and is now set down at the right hand of the Majesty in the heavens.

What is the force of that word "being"—"being the brightness"? He being the brightness of the glory of God has done something. *Since* he is the brightness, *because* he is the brightness of the Father's glory, *because* he is the very image of God, *because* he upholds all things by the word of his power, he has purged our sins. Does it say he *will* purge our sins?—No, it says he has done it. He has cleansed, rinsed, washed them. He hath loved us and washed us in his own blood.

Now, there is a word in the text that really ought not to be there. It is not indicated in the best Greek texts. It is "our." What has Christ done?—Purged sins. He "made purification of sins." Why was it that he by himself should purge sin?—Because he bears all things himself—because in him all things consist—he has by himself purged sin, and made a purification of sin. How long, then, shall we wait for pardon? How long shall we wait to know the complete and perfect forgiveness and cleansing from sin?—Long enough to confess it—to take a thing that is already done. How much sin has he purged?—All sin. Then it is true as a matter of fact, that he has purged our sin. He has purged the sins of all the world, because he came himself to bear all things.

Now Christ has a place better than that of the angels; that better place is that he is set down at the right hand of the Majesty in the heavens; being made so much better than the angels, because he had by inheritance obtained a more excellent name than they. That more excellent name that he has obtained is "Son," which name God had never applied to any of the angels.

All the angels of God worshiped him, the first begotten, when he was brought into the world, so that of Christ in the very lowest place, even in the manger, God said: "Let all the angels of God worship him."

"Thy throne, O God, is forever." These words were addressed by the Father to the Son. "A scepter of righteousness is the scepter of thy kingdom." What is the word which stands as a symbol of power and authority in the kingdom?—Scepter. A scepter means power, so the very nature and power of his kingdom is righteousness. "The kingdom of God is not meat and drink; but righteousness." The scepter of his kingdom is the scepter of righteousness. The power of Christ's kingdom is the power of righteousness. He has loved righteousness, and loving righteousness he has hated iniquity. There is but one state of mind involved in loving righteousness and hating iniquity. If a man loves righteousness, it is not necessary for him to conjure up some other state of mind in order to hate wickedness. It is all in the loving of righteousness. Mark which comes first—love righteousness, hate iniquity. It is a very common thing in this world for people to try to manufacture a love of righteousness, or a sentiment of love of righteousness, by crying out against iniquity; but that is not the way. No, first of all love righteousness, and hating iniquity necessarily follows. "Therefore God, even thy God, hath anointed thee with the oil of gladness above thy fellows,"—in the presence of thy fellows or associates.

We have two things told us here about the kingdom of Christ: the scepter or power, and therefore the nature of his kingdom, is righteousness; and God has anointed him. What does anointing signify?—It signifies kingship. When he was anointed, he was anointed as king. God in anointing him king of this kingdom of righteousness used the oil of gladness; therefore his kingdom is a kingdom of joy. "The kingdom of God is righteousness, and peace, and joy in the Holy Ghost." Those therefore who acknowledge the power of this kingdom will first of all be righteous people. "Thy children shall be all righteous." There can be no question whether those who acknowledge the authority of Christ will be righteous.

The authority is righteous, and whoever acknowledges that authority must be righteous.

But Christ's right to the kingdom, as in the case of an earthly ruler, is demonstrated and sealed by his anointing. That is the thing which inducts him into the kingdom, and establishes him over the kingdom. He is anointed with the oil of gladness, the oil of joy; therefore, since that is the thing which marks his right to rule, his kingdom is a kingdom of joy. Since it is a kingdom of joy and gladness, those that belong to it will rejoice in God, will be joyful in the Lord, joy in the Holy Ghost. Can one, then, be a subject, a loyal subject, of Christ the king, and not be joyful?—No. Then if one is not joyful, there is something the matter. He is not recognizing the authority of the King.

Now, in the second chapter of first John, sixth verse, is a text that we have often read: "He that saith he abideth in him ought himself also so to walk, even as he walked." Does it say obligation is laid upon him to walk as Christ walked? that he should make himself walk as he walked? Let us illustrate: We pass by a field, and we see a tree in the distance. Some one asks me what kind of a tree it is. I have heard that it is a beech tree. He says, If it is a beech tree, then it ought to have a certain shaped leaf, and a peculiar kind of bark. Does he mean that if that is a beech tree, it is the duty of that tree to get some leaves of that kind and put on?—No; if it is a beech tree, that is what it ought to have, because it must have that if it is that kind of tree. Suppose it is not a beech tree, then it ought not to have that kind. He that saith he abideth in Christ ought to walk as he does. That is, if a man says he is a Christian, he ought to have certain distinguishing characteristics. He ought to walk as Christ walked. Why ought he to do so?—Because he is a Christian,—because that kind of walk is characteristic of Christ. He abides in Christ, and he walks as he did; but if he is not like Christ, he is not abiding in Christ.

There are many people who think that the subjects of Christ ought to be glad, and so they try to be glad. Suppose we say, Let us be glad this afternoon. But you can't be glad unless you are glad, and if you are not glad, then you cannot make yourself glad. A bird sings because it is glad—because gladness is in it.

Question: Now upon this point of being always joyful. We read in 1Pet.1:4,5, that we are begotten "to an inheritance incorruptible, and undefiled, and that fadeth not away, reserved in heaven for you, who are kept by the power of God through faith unto salvation ready to be revealed in the last time. Wherein ye greatly rejoice, though now for a season, if need be, ye are in heaviness through manifold temptations." Is there not sorrow at times?

Well, read right on, and it will tell it: "That the trial of your faith, being much more precious than of gold that perisheth, though it be tried with fire, might be found unto praise and honor and glory at the appearing of Jesus Christ: whom having not seen, ye love; in whom, though now ye see him not, yet believing, ye rejoice with joy unspeakable and full of glory."

Here is the blessedness of the peace and joy of Christ, that you do not have to manufacture it. You cannot manufacture it. "Peace I leave with you, my peace I give unto you." Has he given it to everybody here?—Yes. It does not make any difference whether they will take it or not. He has given it.

Now, here is a nickel. Brother Hyatt, I will give that to you for friendship's sake. [Coin laid on table beside him.] Have I given it to him? He has not taken it; I do not know whether he will take it or not; but I have given it to him as a bona fide gift, and I leave it there with him, and I will never take it up again. Now, if you believe that I tell the truth, you believe that I have given him five cents.

Jesus says, "Peace I leave with you, my peace I give unto you." To whom?—To everybody; and he has given it to us. There are some people that do not believe he has given it, and they do not take it, and there are some people who do not want it; but the fact remains that God has given his peace. But what about that peace? "My peace,"—the peace of God, which passeth all understanding. Read further than that: "Not as the world giveth, give I unto you. Let not your heart be troubled, neither let it be afraid." Do not worry. What was the characteristic of Christ's peace? Some think that peace is a sort of happy-go-lucky feeling of complacency, an easy sort of lazy feeling, because the man does not have anything to prod him, and he lies in a hammock in the sunshine, and he has peace,—nothing to do, nothing to worry him. He is a man of peace. That is what men think of peace. That is not the way Christ did. From the cradle to the grave, the devil was seeking every possible opportunity to take his life. He had him in his hands once; that is, his agents did. They took him to the brow of the hill, and they thought they could end his life; and that very thing was being tried continually. But that was not the worst thing he had to bear. The scribes and Pharisees were continually nagging him, criticizing every word he uttered. He had lies told about him. They said, He has a devil; he is crazy; he is a fanatic; he deceives the people; he is leading them astray. And those things he had to endure. And not only his enemies, but even his brethren did not believe on him. And so wherever he went he found trouble always,—something to oppose him, something to come upon him. He was always in turmoil, he was always in trouble; but he was never troubled.

"In the world ye shall have tribulation," but do not be troubled. Christ's gift is of such a nature that a man can have trouble, and not be troubled; he can have affliction and sorrow, and not be sorrowful; he can have heaviness, and yet rejoice; he can have warfare, and be at peace. That is the peace that he gives.

No one was allowed to make any oil like the oil with which the priests were anointed. What do we learn from that? That was not merely an arbitrary thing. Do not try to counterfeit the grace of God. God gives the oil of joy. Do not try to manufacture an artificial joy. It was to show that it could not be done.

Now, continuing the study in Hebrews: "Thou, Lord, in the beginning hast laid the foundation of the earth; and the heavens are the works of thine hands; they shall perish, but thou remainest; and they all shall wax old as doth a garment; and as a vesture shalt thou fold them up, and they shall be changed; but thou art the same, and thy years shall not fail." The heavens and the earth shall grow old, they get old. What is their condition now? Old, worn-out, barren, bald we find the earth in many spots. It is worn out and grown old, so old that it trembles. It did not shake in the beginning when it was new, but now the earth shakes and trembles.

The earth shall wax old like a garment, shall be changed like a vesture. When a garment gets old you lay it aside. When you change an old coat, what do you have?—A new one. The earth and the heavens shall wax old like a garment, and they shall be changed; and then, of course, when they are old and are changed, the new heavens and earth will appear. "But thou art the same, and thy years shall not fail." He does not get old. What a world of comfort there is in that! We change; He is the same. Though we believe not, he is the same. He abideth faithful, always the same. The devil makes us think that Christ changes as we change. But he is the same.

My ministering brethren, seek Jesus with all lowliness and meekness. Do not try to draw the attention of the people to yourselves. Let them lose sight of the instrument, while you exalt Jesus. Talk of Jesus; lose self in Jesus. There is too much bustle and stir about our religion, while Calvary and the cross are forgotten.—Test. No. 31.

Study Number Three
(Thursday Afternoon, February 11, 1897)

We should keep in mind the statements of the first chapter, because the second chapter depends upon the first, and the third chapter depends upon the second, and so on. Let the chapter divisions drop out as you study.

Before beginning where we left off yesterday, let us remember from the first chapter that God speaks in his Son, who is so much higher than the angels, high as they are, powerful as they are; that he sits at the right hand of God. Their work is to minister. They have been sent to men with messages from the Lord, with commandments and directions from the Lord. We read of that in the Old Testament, and whenever those commandments were disobeyed, those directions disregarded, every transgression and disobedience received a just recompense of reward.

But what does the Son speak to us?—Great salvation. Salvation began to be spoken by the Lord, and was brought to us, and confirmed by them that heard it.

Christ was upon the earth; his lips moved; men saw his lips move, and they wondered at the gracious words that proceeded out of his mouth. God was speaking. How often you hear these words: "I do not speak of myself; I have not spoken of myself." God was in Christ speaking the word of reconciliation. Now Christ is gone above, and in his stead, as his representatives, he has put into us the word of reconciliation. Now who said that? Have I said it?—No, the Word says it. Then do not think of it as anything that you have heard me say; but here you read it, and you read it again, and read it alone at home, and when you read it, do not read Brother Kilgore, or Brother Loughborough, or Brother Olsen, or other ministers in there. It does not say the preachers. Who is he talking about here?—"If *any* man be in Christ." Then it is any man that is in Christ. God has put into him the word of reconciliation. And we want to understand that here is the lesson for us today—that God does not know anything about classes and masses, and in the church he does not have high and low. But he has men, and they are all men: and to every one, according to his several ability, God has given the word of reconciliation. And it does not rest upon this man who is a preacher, any more than it does upon you, except as God may have given him greater ability and a wider field. The Word is one and the same for every individual who is in Christ, and that Word is the word of reconciliation. "Therefore if *any* man speak, let him speak as the oracles of God." And he can do it too, if he allows God to speak in him, not his own word, but the Word of God.

I thank God so often when I see and hear of the controversy about the priesthood in the churches that claim to have a sacrificing priesthood, and a clergy who have the right to speak the word,—I thank the Lord that he says to every one of his people, "Ye are a kingdom of priests, to offer up spiritual sacrifices."

We read this morning, from the Testimonies, "The work of saving human souls is an interest infinitely above any other line of work in our world." And when we think of the last verse of the first chapter of Hebrews, we can get some idea of the infinite worth of that work. Angels who excel in strength, angels whose might is that of the mighty winds, God has commissioned to be servants of those who have this work committed to them of saving souls. It is wonderful to think of. It is humiliating to me, and makes me feel ashamed to think how lightly I have esteemed it; to think that God has given to us the work of proclaiming the gospel, while these wondrous beings are ministers to us. He has committed unto us the word of reconciliation, even that same word that Christ proclaimed. And there is given unto us on this earth the identical work that Christ had. For "we pray you *in Christ's stead* be ye reconciled to God." And Christ has given to those mighty beings, simply the work of waiting upon, serving, helping us to whom this ministry is given.

There is something marvelous and altogether unnatural, unworldly, about the gift of God; for when he puts a man in high position—and he has put every one of us in a high position—it does not exalt him, but it humbles him. When the world puts a man in a high position, it exalts him. Why has not God given the angels the work of preaching the gospel and saving souls?—Because he has not put the world to come in subjection unto angels. Here is some glorious comfort for every one to whom God has committed the work of saving souls. Those who hear Christ, proclaim it with the power of God's witnesses,—miracles, signs, and the gift of the Holy Ghost. He has given the teaching of the Gospel to men. He has put the world to come in subjection unto men. And it is an infinitely high work that God gives to man.—

What is man that thou are mindful of him? Or the son of man that thou visitest him? Thou madest him a little lower than the angels; and crownedst him with glory and honor, and didst set him over the works of thy hands.

Where do we find that testified?—In the first chapter of Genesis, and the eighth Psalm. Just think of those two passages; they are doubtless familiar. The Lord said:—

Let us make man in our image, after our likeness; and let them have dominion over the fish of the sea, and over the fowl of the air, and over the cattle, and over all the earth, and over every creeping thing that creepeth upon the earth.

Note each statement. Let them have dominion over the fish of the sea, over the fowl of the air, and over the cattle, and over all the earth, and every creeping thing. And it was so. So God did it. The Psalm says:—

What is man that thou art mindful of him? And the son of man, that thou visitest him? For thou hast made him a little lower than the angels, and hast crowned him with glory and honor. Thou madest him to have dominion over the works of thy hands; thou hast put all things under his feet; all sheep and oxen, yea, and the beasts of the field; the fowl of the air, and the fish of the sea, and whatsoever passeth through the paths of the sea.

There is complete dominion given to man. "For in that he put all things in subjection under him, he left not anything that was not put under him." We see that God gave Adam dominion over all the earth. Does that mean that God took a back seat, and abdicated in favor of man?—No. God could not give up his right, because all things existed only in him. It is the Word of God that upholds all things. And it is his power that rules all things. Therefore the dominion which God gave to Adam over all the earth, over the birds and beasts and fishes, was just as complete as God's power, just as complete as God's dominion; for he was ruling in Adam. All things stand by his Word. He spoke, and it was. So when we look abroad on the things of nature, we see evidences of his power. When we look over the meadow, we see the Word of God made grass. God spake, and, lo! that Word appeared as a tree, or as grass.

You may have seen pictures of voice forms, even human voice forms, that when a note would be uttered so that the breath which formed that note would impinge upon a membrane upon which were particles of sand, in every instance the sand that was set in motion by the vibration took different forms, shapes of things. This is simply an illustration, just a hint of the fact that God "spake and it *was.*" God spake, and his voice took all the infinite forms that we see in nature; and everything that we see, and every spot that our foot treads upon, was given by God to let us know that his Word is something, and not mere emptiness.

As the last act of creation, God made man. And as in all creation we see the Word of God made trees, grass, etc., in man we see the Word of God made flesh. He was the son of God. We find that in the third chapter of Luke. Sometimes we think those genealogies are pretty dry things, but the point of it all is in the very last word.

So here we stand looking at what ought to be, for we know that whatsoever God does, it shall be forever. Nothing can be added to it, nothing taken away from it. Now we are looking still, and we see man there, with all that God gave him. Now what next does the text say?—"Now we see not yet all things put under him." Fallen as nature is, God has absolute control over the beasts and birds and fishes; even yet they will do his will. They do it as far as man will let them. Man is the only being that will not yield perfect obedience. And it is man's interference and rebellion that stops them from obeying Him. We are looking at the earth; but what earth is it that was given to man?—The world to come. So unto the angels has he not put into subjection the world to come, but he has put it under subjection to man. That dominion which man had in the beginning over the beasts and birds and fishes, and over the earth, is the dominion which God has given to man over the world to come. So that in the world to come man again will have that complete and perfect dominion over everything that God has made; all will be subject to him as unto God, subject to him as head, because God is in him, and God will be all in all. Then the Word will be made flesh in its perfection just as it was in the beginning in Adam. "But now we see not yet all things put under him;" but on the contrary, we see just the reverse. In the first place, all things were put under man; in the next place, man is under all things. In the first place, man was on the top; now he is under. Fallen man has everything on him. He is bound hand and foot, delivered over to Satan; he is fallen. So while we are looking at man in the noble position in which he was made in the beginning, as we still look at him we see Jesus; because in the beginning the Word was made flesh, and so it is Christ, the Word, in Adam. There we see Jesus. Where?—Just in the same place where man fell; there we see Jesus, made a little lower than the angels because he took man's place. When, in the beginning he was infinitely higher, for the suffering of death, to rescue man, to save man, to raise him up, he took his place. Now, if one will lift up another who falls, he must go where the man is. Wherever there is a fallen man, Jesus is there. But I am a fallen man, too. Just let each one of us take that to himself. The Lord has not cast off man. We read, "For the Lord will not cast off forever." He does not cast off at all. No; man takes himself away; God does not cast off. And there is nobody that can pluck man out of his hands. There we are safe as long as we are willing to abide in him.

 We see man perfect, with dominion; then fallen, with everything above him, and on him, and against him. Looking still there, we see Jesus as man, and for the suffering of death we see him crowned with glory and honor; that, by the grace of God, he should taste death for every man. Therefore, wherever you see a man fallen,—and he cannot fall lower than into the grave,—there you see Christ, who went into the grave and tasted the depths of sin and degradation for every man. So every man's degradation and sin is on Christ—the man Christ Jesus. But the same man Christ Jesus is crowned with glory and honor. Now mark: A crown signifies a king or ruler. Where in this chapter have we first read about a crown? "But one in a certain place testified, saying, What is man, that thou art mindful of him? or the son of man, that thou visitest him? Thou madest him a little lower than the angels; and crownedst him with glory and honor." That is to say, you have made him king, a king of glory. Adam, the king of glory and honor; so long was he over all things. But when he sinned, then he lost the glory he had. But now we see Jesus crowned with glory and honor, and in the position that man was in, in the beginning. But he is crowned with glory and honor in the same nature as man had. So just as God made man, and crowned him with glory and honor, we now see the man Jesus, that Man who is in every man crowned with honor and glory; and he added all things unto him.

Now read the last words of the first chapter of Ephesians:—

That the God of our Lord Jesus Christ, the Father of glory, may give unto you the spirit of wisdom and revelation in the knowledge of him; the eyes of your understanding being enlightened; that ye may know what is the hope of his calling, and what the riches of the glory of his inheritance in the saints, and what is the exceeding greatness of his power to usward who believe, according to the working of his mighty power, which he wrought in Christ, when he raised him from the dead, and set him at his own right hand in the heavenly places far above all principality, and power, and might, and dominion, and every name that is named, not only in this world, but also in that which is to come. Verses 17–21.

But what was the name which Jesus always delighted to give himself while upon this earth?—The Son of man. The Son of man is come to seek and to save that which was lost. When ye hath delivered the Son of man. The Son of man shall go to Jerusalem, and they shall crucify him, and he shall be buried. And on the third day the Son of man shall rise again. But and if ye shall see the Son of man. Ye shall see the Son of man coming in the clouds of heaven. All this time it is the "Son of man." And this Son of man we see, because of his faithfulness, crowned with glory and honor, and having under him all principalities and powers and might and dominion, not only in this world, but also in the world to come. For unto the angels hath he not put under subjection the world to come, but he hath put the world to come in subjection to man, even Jesus, and ye are complete in him. Read in the second chapter, verses 1–6:—

And you hath he quickened, who were dead in trespasses and sins; wherein in time past ye walked according to the course of this world, according to the prince of the power of the air, the spirit that now worketh in the children of disobedience: among whom also we all had our conversation in times past in the lusts of our flesh, fulfilling the desires of the flesh and of the mind; and were by nature the children of wrath, even as others. But God, who is rich in mercy, for his great love wherewith he loved us, even when we were dead in sins, hath quickened us together with Christ, (by grace ye are saved;) and hath raised us up together, and made us sit together in heavenly places in Christ Jesus.

Where is he?—Far above all principalities and powers. Is not the work of saving souls far above everything else in this world? It has been said that "to be a Roman is greater than to be a king." In this day, and in every age, to be a Christian is greater than to be a king of this earth. And now we have that Word confirmed unto us by them that heard him, "God also bearing them witness, both with signs and wonders, and with divers miracles, and gifts of the Holy Ghost," according to his power, because under the angels he had not put in subjection the world to come whereof we speak. That simply says that the power, the honor, the glory, the dignity to accompany the preaching of the gospel which God has put into those who are reconciled to him, is the power and glory of the world to come.

Study Number Four
(Friday Afternoon, February 12, 1897)

What contrast in words is there in the beginning of this second chapter of Hebrews? The word of the Lord, and the word of the angels; and the word of the angels was steadfast. But what is the difference between the word spoken by the angels and the word spoken by the Lord? What word does the Lord speak?—Salvation. Did the angels speak that word?—No. See what the text says: "If the word spoken by angels was steadfast, and every transgression and disobedience received a just recompense of reward," then every neglect, every transgression, and every disobedience of the word which the angels spoke received a recompense of reward.

Now, what is the contrast? "How shall we escape if we neglect so great salvation?" And this great salvation was first spoken by the Lord, and then confirmed unto us by them that heard him.

Where do the angels come in in this work of salvation? They have a place, but not any place in the line of carrying the word. It first began to be spoken by the Lord, and then comes to us by them that heard it. Now, where do the angels come in in this spreading abroad of the word?—They do not come in. But what is their relation to it?—They are ministering servants,—waiters upon those who carry this word; and I say again, as I said yesterday, there comes over me every time I think of it, a most wonderful feeling of awe; it frightens me. And yet I am glad to think of the wonderful work committed to man, a work so great—just think of it! We need to dwell upon that to realize the glory of this ministry.

Now, that does not say that we are great. It is not saying that we are above the angels, because we are doing a work which is not committed to them, and a work that they cannot do. That work of salvation is spoken only by the Lord and them that hear him, but not by angels, because under them he hath not put into subjection the world to come. Then this proclamation of the word of salvation has an intimate relation with the world to come. And what is this world to come whereof we speak?—A new heavens and a new earth; the world has been put into subjection to man, according to the testimony of one who testified in a certain place about man, saying, "What is man, that thou art mindful of him? or the son of man that thou visitest him? Thou madest him a little lower than the angels; thou crownedst him with glory and honor." A crown signifies a king; therefore when God made man he made him a king. He wore a crown of glory, signifying a kingdom of glory. O, the whole earth was full of the glory of God undimmed. Then man was a king of glory, and his kingdom was the earth. All things were put under him. There was nothing that was not put under him. Every living thing was put under him, and he was the ruler over all, and the earth itself was in subjection to him. But the power back of and in it all was God's power, for God alone has power.

Man was made in the image of God, of the dust of the earth. "The Lord God formed man dust," literally, not formed him of the dust, but formed him dust. He then breathed into his nostrils the breath of life, and man became a living soul. But the man was dust, and after he was crowned with glory and honor he was nothing but dust. Now this dust that God took and formed into this shape, and crowned with glory and honor, he put over the works of his hands put under him all things, gave him dominion over all things; and so it was dust that had dominion over all things. He was still dust; and how much more power had this dust that was formed in this figure than that dust that still lay on the ground?—It had no more power. And that is demonstrated in the fact that when the breath which God puts in there is gone, it is just as helpless as it was before, or as that other dust. Then the power is not in the dust; and here is just where the world—all mankind—make the mistake. Man sees his face and form in the mirror, and admires himself, and he will not believe that he is dust; or, if he does acknowledge that he is dust, it is a different kind of dust than any other kind. The failure to recognize this is what makes one man assume lordship over another, to think himself better than another man; and the Lord wants us to keep to first principles all the time. Man at the best is nothing but dust. We cannot dwell upon that too much, because the forgetting of it is what led to all sin in the beginning. Satan said to Eve that she would become like God. Now, if she had remembered the Word, and her origin, could she have supposed that that would be true?—No. It is the forgetting of it that lifts up man and makes him proud. Man in his highest state is nothing but dust.

What is the difference between that dust thrown out there, and this here? God has chosen to use this dust in a little different way from what he uses that dust. God had a purpose in that dust; it is worth something; it will produce fruit. Here is dust that God has caused to bring forth another kind of fruit. How much more right has this dust that can walk about instead of being blown about by the wind, to boast of what it does than that dust out there in the field has. Out there you will see some beautiful, fine, rosy-cheeked apples. But it is not supposable that that dust in the field should begin to boast: Why, I am better than that dust in the road; that dust in the road does not do any good, but lies there day after day, and does not accomplish anything. See what I have done. And yet it has just as much right to do that as we have to boast of anything we have done.

Here is a lesson of encouragement of what God can do. Man, placed over the works of God's hands, crowned with glory and honor—only dust still—is an evidence of the power of God.

But now looking at that inanimate dust with all things put under him, what is the next thing we see?—The next thing is that all things are not under him. Still looking at that; what do we see?—We see Jesus. We see him made a little lower than the angels, right down where man fell. What has he now?—A crown of glory and honor. But before he got that crown of glory and honor, what did he have?—He took death; he tasted death.

First, we see man crowned with glory and honor, having dominion over the works of God, everything under him. We keep on looking, and we see not all things under him, but instead, we see Jesus down at the very place where man fell; and we keep on looking, and next we see him crowned with glory and honor. That is the order. He was made a little lower than the angels; he was man. So that when we consider him now, we consider him as man, and from this point through we have Jesus before us all the time, but always as man. Never forget that. When man in the beginning was made a little lower than the angels, and then Jesus made a little lower than the angels, what was the difference?—There is none. When God made Adam by his Word, the Word was made flesh. As God spoke all things into existence, his words went forth, and, lo! the earth appeared. His Word went forth; he spoke; he said, Trees, and they were there; he said, Grass, and it was; so that all these things that grow over the ground are visible manifestations of the Word. It is the Word of life, and these are simply some of the various forms of the life of the Word. And so with man formed there in the beginning. There we see the Word manifested as flesh. The power by which this was done was God's power, and so God was in the Word, and the Word was in Adam, so that this power could be manifested in him, God dwelling in him and working in him; God taking this dust and using it to do these wonderful things. It is God that worketh in you to will and to do his good pleasure. Now, if God is there, and I am here, that is altogether too far away. It is God that worketh in me. The Word was made flesh, and the life of Adam was the life of God. He has no other life. Now the blessedness of this is, when man fell, the Word was made flesh. But suppose God had forsaken him, and had not been willing to make the Word flesh; what would have become of him?—He would have returned to dust. But God continues his life to man. So when man fell, God goes right down there with him. Is that so, or is it some fancy? Did God continue life to man, notwithstanding he had sinned? We are here, are we not? We are sinners. We are living, are we not? Whose life is it manifested in us?—It is God's life. Then God continues his life to sinful men. When sin entered, death came; so when man sinned, death came upon him. God stayed with him; therefore, in that he stayed with man, although man had sinned, God took upon himself sinful flesh. And so he took upon himself death, for death had passed upon all the world.

Now, let us see further. All creation is continued until now "by the same Word." Everything in this world is kept by the same Word. Although everything is cursed, and everybody can see that, it is yet a fact that it continues; it is an evidence that God is there, Christ is there, the divine Word is there bearing the curse. But in what thing does Christ endure the curse? Where is that point where the curse falls upon Christ?—Sinful flesh. Not only sinful flesh, but that which stands as the symbol of the curse that falls upon Christ—the cross. What is the evidence that he bears the curse?—"Accursed is every one that hangeth on a tree." Death and the cross both together mean the curse; therefore wherever there is anything, there is the curse. Nevertheless, wherever there is anything, there is Christ. Wherever there is anything, then, that exists and bears the curse, there is Christ. But where Christ has the curse upon him, he bears the cross. Then do you not see the truthfulness of that statement which appeared from Sister White about a year ago, that "the cross of Christ is stamped upon every leaf in the forest?" And a little later than a year ago there appeared in a first-page article of the *Review and Herald* a statement that the very bread we eat is stamped with the cross. There is something wonderful in that. Perhaps when you read that in every blade, and every leaf, there is the cross of Christ, some of us read it over without thinking about it, and some of us simply said, with Nicodemus, how can this be? How soon do we find Christ crucified, then?—Just as soon as there was any curse. And he is risen again as well, because if you preach Christ crucified, his resurrection necessarily goes with that.

Now, see how God has proclaimed the gospel for our encouragement everywhere. People are inclined to get discouraged; Christians are likely to think, Well, the Lord has forgotten us. Did you ever think that way, as though the Lord didn't care for you;—that he has left you alone? Is there any one who has not felt that way, discouraged, in short? I am not of much importance in this world, we sometimes say; I am of no consequence; I am only one very insignificant and despised, and justly despised; I could drop out, and it wouldn't make any difference. He said that not a sparrow can fall to the ground without his notice; and why?—Because the life of God is there, and there is nothing that can come upon anything in this world that God does not feel. It touches him personally, because his life is all the sensibility that there is in this world. You are struck, you are beaten; you feel it. What makes you feel it? If you were dead you wouldn't feel it. Why do you feel it?—Because you are alive. Where do you get life?—It comes from God. It is God's own life isn't it? Then is it possible for a human being to be touched, just touched—not beaten, bruised, or despised—and the Lord not feel it? Can it be so, whether saint or sinner? Can anything happen to any creature in this world does God not feel? Whither shall I go from his presence, and where shall

I go to be away from the presence of God? We cannot get away, because God's power is in everything; and therefore a sparrow cannot fall to the ground without the Lord knowing it. We live with all these infirmities. That is Christ in the flesh, then. Do you suppose that Christ would have endured all this, and stayed here all these years, with all this infirmity and wickedness and weakness and sin upon him, and then by and by step out and let it all drop? If he was to do that, he would have let it drop in the beginning; but the fact that he came in fallen humanity is an evidence of God's presence, and his presence to give life. And so God on everything has put the stamp of the cross,—upon every leaf, upon every blade of grass, upon everything that we have to do with. He simply means that everywhere we go, and everything we have to do, and everything we eat, and the air we breathe,—through these he is simply preaching the gospel to us, giving the gospel to us. Encouragement, strength, salvation!

"LIKE the roads of the South, the path of duty is hedged with everblooms, pure, and white as snow. It is only when we turn to the right or left that we are pierced by thorns, and concealed dangers."

Study Number Five
(Sunday Afternoon, February 14, 1897)

Our text reads: "What is man, that thou art mindful of him? or the Son of man, that thou visitest him? Thou madest him a little lower than the angels," etc. Here we are referred to the origin of man. When we read that God made man, to what are our minds instantly turned?—To the record in Gen.2:7: "And the Lord God formed man of the dust of the ground."

Wherever in the Old Testament it speaks of any one being broken to pieces by the Lord, we find coupled with that repentance, submission, or bitterness of soul, dust and ashes. When they humbled themselves before the Lord, they put dust on their heads. What was signified in this?—I am nothing but dust. In the fifty-first, the penitential Psalm, it says near the close: "The sacrifices of God are a broken spirit; a broken and a contrite heart, O God, than wilt not despise." That word "contrite" means rubbed together until it is dust. The Lord, then, does not despise dust; because he can do a great deal even with dust. A good workman does not despise his material. Dust is one of the things which the Lord takes to do everything. Out of dust he made all things to grow. Out of dust he made man to rule over the works of his hands, therefore the Lord does not despise dust.

In Psalms 90:1–3, we read:—

Thou hast been our dwelling-place in all generations. Before the mountains were brought forth, or ever thou hadst formed the earth and the world, even from everlasting to everlasting, thou art God. Thou turnest man to destruction; and sayest, return, ye children of men.

The better reading is, "Thou turnest man to dust." The original word is the same as that before translated dust. It does not mean, turning man to destruction, for that would reduce him to a condition from which he could not be brought back. The force, then, of this expression is, that to turn man to dust has something to do with salvation. The Lord turns man to dust in order to make him over. Thus he turns him to dust, and says, "Return, ye children of men." When God sends the message of reproof, that breaks a man all to pieces, and gives him a broken and contrite heart. Then he is just where the Lord can create him a new man. But if a man does not believe this message which breaks him all to pieces, he becomes discouraged, and says, I am good for nothing.

Here is a man that knows himself to be a sinner, but he does not and will not believe that he can be anything different. All the talk about what God is able to do for him, and to make of him, is to him as an idle tale; he doesn't believe that God can make him a righteous man, although he is contrite. That man may think he believes the Bible, but the fact is he does not believe the simple statement that the Lord can form man of the dust of the earth. Or if he does believe that, he believes that the Lord has lost his power since doing it the first time, and cannot do it again. But the Lord did that thing once, and he has not forgotten how. In the beginning he made man of dust. Now the man that doubts that God can take him where he is, and do what he pleases with him, does not believe that simple statement; and he needs to go back and learn the first principles.

I am reminded of an incident: A friend of mine was going through the potteries in England, where thousands of men are employed. Of course you know that in making vessels some will be spoiled. He saw an old man with a barrow full of those broken vessels, and he said, "Uncle, what are you going to do with those?"—"O, I am going to convert `em." And he went up and threw them into a hopper, and they were all ground up, and converted into dust, ready to be made into new vessels. In the first place they were spoiled, and were perverted. Then they were turned to dust again; and new vessels were made of them. The potter was just as able to make new vessels of them as he was to make them in the first instance.

There is a lesson in this that the Lord wants us to learn—that he can make us over again, as well as he made us in the first place. But the trouble is that this dust begins to put on airs, and look down on other dust, and to forget that it is dust, or else to think that it is a little better quality of clay than some other. The man will not allow that he is dust, and he will not allow the Lord to use him. But as long as we acknowledge that we are dust, we have the blessed comfort that the Lord God made man of the dust of the earth, and crowned him with glory and honor, and set him over the works of his hands, and put all things in subjection under his feet; and that what God did in the beginning, he is able to do still, and does do it in the man Christ Jesus. The text shows us two things at once—utter helplessness and wonderful dignity. The dignity comes only because of helplessness. The lowest places mean high places with God.

God in the beginning made man of dust, and gave him dominion over everything. When God does anything, he does not undo it; and when he makes a gift, he does not take it back. God gave the earth to man, and he has not taken it back; it belongs to man forever. What world is it which God has given to man?—The world to come. What about this world? This is not the one. What does he say about us in this world?—"He gave himself for us, that he might deliver us from this present evil world." What condition is it that calls for deliverance?—Bondage. The whole thing is turned upside down. In the beginning man had dominion, and now he has to be delivered from the thing which he ruled. "Ye are not of this world, but I have chosen you out of" it.

What is the only use, then, that the child of God has for this world?—It is only just a place to stop while waiting for the world to come. It is only a steppingstone, which he is to get off from. Who has this world?—The devil is the only one. Often the professed people of God, who have a home and a right in the earth made new, and are heirs to the kingdom which God has promised to them that love him, try to get a foothold in the affairs of this world, which the men of the earth are always trying to do. While professing to be heirs to the kingdom of God, they are trying to share a second dominion, and get a part of the devil's dominion. Now, there is a message which has been sent. I will not read it, but it is in regard to the people of God taking part in the turmoil and politics of this world. The word politics has nothing to do with Christ. There is no politics with God. Policy and politics go together, but God has nothing to do with policy. If we had read the Bible and believed the truth, it would not have been necessary for a message to be sent. It is the world to come that God has given to us, and God has sent Jesus to deliver men from this present evil world. Christ is the Word made flesh, made lower than the angels, that he, by the grace of God, should taste death for every man. By what comes death?—Sin. So he took upon himself sin. Man was made just as good in the beginning as the Lord knew how to make him. He was made perfect. The devil said, I will spoil that man; I will show that I am stronger than the Lord.

The Lord made man to rule over the works of his hands. Satan said, I have spoiled his plan; it cannot be done. The Lord said, Yes, it can; and not only that, but I will take a fallen man, with all his infirmities, and I will rule the world through even him. The devil is defeated. That is not a theory; it is practical for you and me. When the devil has me down, he cannot rejoice against me; for when I fall I shall rise again. And just as low as I fall, just so high I will rise above where I was before. The Word was made perfect flesh in Adam, but in Christ was the Word made fallen flesh. Christ goes down to the bottom, and there is the Word flesh, sinful flesh. Who has believed our report? To whom has the arm of the Lord been revealed? There is no form nor comeliness in him, nothing that we should desire in him. Who would believe that he could see him, that same being,—so marred, more than any man,—crowned with glory and honor. What goes with the crowning of glory and honor?—Kingship. Of what?—Glory. Of what?—Of the world to come. Then the man Christ Jesus has a right now to the world to come. In the beginning it was the Lord ruling through Adam; now it is the Lord ruling through the second Adam, and through far inferior conditions, doing what he would have done through the first Adam under the first conditions. This is the glory connected with what we read the other day in the first of Ephesians:—

The eyes of your understanding being enlightened; that ye may know what is the hope of his calling, and what the riches of the glory of his inheritance in the saints, and what is the exceeding greatness of his power to us-ward who believe, according to the working of his mighty power, which he wrought in Christ, when he raised him from the dead, and set him at his own right hand in the heavenly places, far above all principality, and power, and might, and dominion, and every name that is named, not only in this world, but also in that which is to come.

Who is it that has all this?—The *man* Christ Jesus. And you also hath he made alive in Christ, and hath raised us up with him, and made us to sit together in heavenly places in Christ Jesus. Unto the angels hath he not put in subjection the world to come, but he has to us; and that is the reason why the angels cannot preach the gospel. The heavens belong to the Lord our God; but the earth hath he given to the children of men. One man lost it; Another came and regained it. And he was lifted up; and you hath he lifted up to sit with him in the same place, "far above all principality, and power, and might, and dominion, and every name that is named, not only in this world [that is a small thing], but also in that which is to come."

How much of an idea can a man have of the dignity of his position as a prince of God, an heir of God, and joint-heir with Christ, sharing what Christ has of the world to come, sitting with Christ in heavenly places, if he spends time digging around in the muck-heap of the politics of the world. These two things do not go together. You would not think of the President of the United States running for town-clerk, while still President of the United States. Think of the President of the United States coming down and taking part in a village caucus or running for office in a school district; yet there is a congruity in that, because it is all a part of the same dominion. But here is a man quickened, made alive in Christ, in possession of the power of the world to come, and then taking hold upon this world, from which the Lord said he must be delivered. He says, I know God has made me a ruler over the world, but let me play with this bubble a little while. I know that I am going to leave it, but there is something so inspiring, so thrilling, in the beat of the big drum; so let me play a little while before I leave it.

Brethren, we do not begin to appreciate what the Lord has for us. That comes by the spirit of wisdom and revelation in the knowledge of him. We need to pray for the Spirit of God; praying that we may know the high calling and the riches of the glory of the inheritance. The man who has found a diamond mine, and knows the value of it, does not have to be pleaded with not to put clay in his pockets, in place of the diamonds. But the trouble with us is, we have gone daft. We have not come to our senses. We have not received the spirit of wisdom and revelation in the knowledge of Christ, so that we can appreciate the inheritance that God has given us.

The things that are seen, are not real; they pass away in a little while. But the things that are not seen, are real. God has given to man only eternal things to deal with; he gave him the eternal world. The center of man's dominion was the garden of Eden; that was his home. No defilement came upon that, so that has continued unsmirched until now, and will so continue to all eternity. The central part, the homestead itself, has never been lost, never been cursed or defiled. And that is the thing we have to deal with; that is where our citizenship is. Some people think that Christians are the ones best qualified to rule in this world, but they are just the ones who are not. This world does not pertain to them, and they should leave the government of it to those to whom it pertains—to those who are of it. God has not given us any citizenship here; he has not given us anything to do with this world, except to get out of it, and take as many people along with us as we can: because it is a sinking ship, and going to perdition, and we are safe here only while we are saving or helping somebody else out.

Study Number Six
(Monday Afternoon, February 15, 1897)

We begin with the ninth verse: "We see Jesus." Where are we looking?

(Voice) "To man in his fallen state."

Yes, our gaze is directed to man's first dominion; as we look we see him fall, and, still looking, we see Jesus taking man's fallen condition, and crowned with glory and honor. We, as well as the rest of the professed Christian world, have been for the most part looking at what is rather than at what ought to be. When we have read of the dealings of God with his people in the Old Testament, we have lost sight of his design for them, and have seen what they took, rather than what God intended them to have. God's design was one thing, and what they took was something else. If they had accepted God's plan, and taken what he had for them, their history would have been vastly different.

God was with them all the time; he did not forsake them; but that was no proof that what they did was right. If it were, that would be an end to any improvement in Christian living whatever. "God has been with me in the past when I kept Sunday," says one. That is all right. "God has been with me, and I won't change." He was with such, but he will not remain with them long if they proceed on that basis. If they think they have nothing still to receive, they are leaving the Lord. The Lord was with Israel that by all means within his power he might lead them to take what he had for them in the beginning.

Now we look at the wonderful dominion that God gave to man, every man, for Jesus in winning it back tasted death for every man,—and that is what we want to look at a great deal,—the completeness of the dominion, the dignity conferred on man. So wonderful was the honor placed on man, that although God himself is the supreme ruler of the universe, his purpose was that he would rule the earth only through man, and that he would not interfere outside of man. But man is dust. And here is a lesson of what God can do through dust. But while looking there we do not now see all things put under man, but we see Jesus—Jesus lower than angels, that is, man. The Word was made flesh. God was manifest in the flesh, in human flesh in the beginning, because the power that worked in Adam was God's power. Then when man sinned, and repudiated God, God did not take him at his word, and leave him alone, but went down with him as low as he fell, and said, Poor man, I will help you; and He stayed with him. So we see Jesus lower than the angels; that is, we see him as man. But we see Him crowned with honor and glory as the son of man. Mark this, it is as the Son of man, not as the Son of God, that we see him crowned with glory and honor. It was not necessary for the Son of God to come to this earth to suffer in order that he might be crowned with glory; for he was the very shining forth of the bright glory of God. But he made himself of no reputation, emptied himself, and became man; took human flesh, in order that man might again be crowned with glory and honor.

"We see Jesus, who was made a little lower than the angels, because of the suffering of death crowned with glory and honor." Notice that in this verse we have the whole of Christ's work for man. We have his humiliation and death, and his resurrection and ascension. When Christ was raised from the dead, how high was he raised? Read again: "The exceeding greatness of his power to usward who believe according to the working of his mighty power, which he wrought in Christ, when he raised him from the dead, and set him at his own right hand in the heavenly places, far above all principality, and power, and might, and dominion, and every name that is named, not only in this world, but also in that which is to come." Eph.1:19–21.

When Christ was raised from the dead he was raised to the throne of God. "And you hath he quickened who were dead in trespasses and sins." He "hath raised us up together with him." Christ was raised from the dead to glory just the same way as when the righteous are raised from the dead they are raised to glory. But even now through the power of the resurrection we are raised with him who sits in heavenly places as the man Christ Jesus. All this was done for Christ as man, for Christ as one of us. There is no question about that. We all understand that. If we do understand it, we understand a great deal.

I do not mean to say we comprehend it, but we understand it in the way that we understand any truth. "By faith we understand." That does not mean to say that we can figure it out and explain it; that cannot be done. That cannot be known even in eternity; it cannot be explained. That is the mystery of God. Only the mind of God can fathom it; only God can understand it; but we can understand it and get the good of it by believing it, and it then becomes a practical experience to us.

Jesus by the grace of God tasted death for every man: "For it became him for whom are all things, and by whom are all things, in bringing many sons unto glory, to make the Captain of their salvation perfect through suffering." It became him; it was a fitting thing; it was a necessary thing, it was exactly the thing to do. Whom did it become? Look closely at that verse. He who brings many sons unto God, makes the Captain of their salvation—Christ—perfect through suffering. So we have in this verse God the Father, the many sons who are brought to glory, and the Captain through whose sufferings they are brought to glory. It became God to make their Captain perfect through sufferings. He tasted death for every man. It was a fitting thing to do, and the only thing that could be done to carry out the original plan of giving the earth to man,—that eternal purpose that could not be changed even by man's fall.

All judgment is committed to the Son, to Christ, not because he is the Son of God, but because he is the Son of man. As we studied a few minutes ago, God has designed (and he does not change his purpose) to rule the world, the dominion which he gave to man,—not this world, but the world to come,—solely through man. Because dominion was given to man, therefore to man is given judgment. But do not forget that God's people are not to rule in this world. It is not this world, but the world to come, that God has put in subjection to man,—a perfect world under the dominion of perfect man. Now just note in passing how the simple truth takes the bottom out of every false theory.

Take the theory that Christians are the people above all others that have the right to rule in this world, because they are the only ones that are fit to rule. But they are the only ones that have no right to rule in this world. They have nothing to do with it. To them is given the world to come. O, let us not be selfish; when God has given to us the world to come, let us not try to rob the people of this world of all the comfort they can get out of it. Do not rob them of it; it is not fair. Instead of Christians being the only ones who are to rule this world, they are the ones who are to keep their hands off. Let those rule it to whom it pertains. To God's people pertains the world to come. Then what have we to do?—Our part is to get away from this world, and to gather into our arms as many poor souls as we can get, and take them along.

So in the pursuance of God's original plan, the dominion being lost by man, man must win it back, because if some other being than man wins it back, then the plan is not carried out. But we say it is God in man. Of course it is, because it was God in man in the beginning. It is God in man all the time. Who could rule the world in the beginning? Man could not rule it; dust could not lift itself up to do anything; but God in man could do all things. So as by man came death, by man came also the resurrection from the dead. O, there is a wonderful honor God has placed upon man, but man must not think that he is God. He is dust, but God's presence in him glorifies him.

"For both he that sanctifieth, and they that are sanctified, are all one." Wherefore Christ is not ashamed to call them brethren. We have seen instances of men who were ashamed of their families—men who, having come into better circumstances, acquired a little bit of learning perhaps, or a little extra money, are ashamed to have it known that they belong to their family. They do, nevertheless; they are the same blood. But he who sanctifies, and they who are sanctified, are all one. Wherefore he is not ashamed to acknowledge the family relation. Do not you see that that binds the Lord Jesus to us, in indissoluble bonds? He acknowledges he is not ashamed to own us as brethren. What is the proof of it?—Saying, "I will declare thy name unto my brethren." To whom is he speaking when he says, I will declare thy name?—Christ speaks to the Father, and says, I will declare thy name unto my brethren. Who is that?—It is we. Is it because we are so good that He is not ashamed to call us brethren? If we were good, would there be any use of saying that he is not ashamed? There must be something that, under ordinary circumstances, would make him ashamed. O, there is enough, under ordinary circumstances, to be ashamed of. But the proof that he is not ashamed is found in the fact that he says, "I will declare thy name unto my brethren."

Now, what condition is it that would make it necessary that Christ should declare God's name to any one? What is the only condition under which he should need to declare the name of the Father?—It is that they do not know the name. There would be no use in declaring the name if they knew it. Then those to whom he declares the name of God, are those who do not know the name of the Father, and they are his brethren. What do we call those who do not know the name of the Lord?—Heathen, are they not? Such we were before we were converted. You can remember the time when you did not know him. I can remember the time when I did not know him any more than if I had been born in the heart of Africa. I had heard the name, but I did not know him. Then those to whom Christ says, I will "declare the name of the Lord," are the heathen people—not necessarily the heathen in Africa, but the heathen in America, or Europe, and all over the world. The Lord says, They are my brethren.

God would bring many sons to glory. He calls them sons. They are his sons, dishonored, disgraced. Adam is said in the genealogy in Luke, to have been the son of God. When he fell, what then?—A fallen son, a prodigal son. The prodigal son took his father's goods, and then went and wasted it: but he was a son nevertheless. The father said, "This, my son, was dead, and is alive; was lost, and is found." So we read, "Behold, what manner of love the Father hath bestowed upon us, that we should be called the sons of God." On whom?—On us—on poor fallen wretches. "Behold, what manner of love the Father hath bestowed upon us." Who?—Me; that I should be called the son of God. That is love. Christ is up there in heaven. We are groping in darkness and ignorance, and he says to the Father, I will go down and declare thy name to my brethren. I will show my brethren who you are. They do not know you. They are aliens and foreigners. They have been misled, and have talked against you; I will go and declare your name to them.

And what is that name? In Ex.34:6,7, we read:—

The Lord God, merciful and gracious, long-suffering, and abundant in goodness and truth, keeping mercy for thousands, forgiving iniquity and transgression and sin.

That is the name of the Lord. "The name of the Lord is a strong tower." Now Christ says, "I will declare thy name unto my brethren." It makes no difference what the color of the skin, where the men are born, what they have done, where they have lived, how poor, despised, and weak. Christ says, I will go and "declare thy name unto my [their] brethren." So every follower of Christ will say, "I will go and declare thy name unto my brethren" in China, in India, in the slums of the city. We will go and declare his name to all of our brethren whom we can find. And that is the only thing that will put life into the missionary work. We are all brethren—there is no such thing as "foreign missionary work." The field is the world. It is all the same field. In one sense we are all foreigners, pilgrims, strangers, in a foreign field; but there is no foreign field in the sense that one part of the world is foreign to the other. Christ regards himself as one with all mankind, and that is why he saves man; and we can really share his work of saving sinners only as we recognize our relation to them.

Take the tenth chapter of Romans for a moment, beginning with the sixth verse: "But the righteousness which is of faith speaketh on this wise, Say not in thine heart, Who shall ascend into heaven? (that is, to bring Christ down from above:) or, Who shall descend into the deep? (that is, to bring up Christ again from the dead.)" This text is quoted from Deut.30:12–14, when Christ is called the "Word:"—

It is not in heaven that thou shouldest say, Who shall go up for us to heaven, and bring unto us, that we may hear it, and do it? Neither is it beyond the sea, that thou shouldest say, Who shall go over the sea for us, and bring it to us, that we may hear it, and do it? But the word is very nigh unto thee, in thy mouth, and in thy heart, that thou mayest do it.

Say not in thy heart, who shall ascend into heaven and bring Christ down. Why not?—Because he is already here. The coming down is the humiliation, the crucifixion: coming down, he humbled himself, and became obedient, even to the death of the cross. Or, say not, who shall descend into the deep, to bring Christ up. Why not?—He has risen. But where is this crucified and risen Christ?—"The Word is nigh thee." How near?—"In thy mouth, and in thy heart; that is, the word of faith, which we preach: that if thou shalt confess with thy mouth the Lord Jesus, and shalt believe in thine heart that God hath raised him from the dead, thou shalt be saved."

What kind of people are addressed when it is said, "Keep these commandments that I command thee this day?

(A voice) "Sinners."

But they say they cannot do it. They may say, I do not know what the commandment is. The word is to those people who do not know it, or if they do know it, they do not do it; at any rate the word comes to sinners. Yes, God sends the word to all peoples, to let them know the eternal truth. He has come here, in the flesh. God is made flesh, and in that flesh he is glorified, because he has tasted death for every man.

Christ has come in the flesh, my flesh. Why? Is it because I am so good?—O, no; for there is no good flesh for Christ to come into. Christ has come in the flesh, in every man's flesh. "That was the true Light, which lighteth every man that cometh into the world." The life is the light, and lights every man. In other words, every man in this world lives upon the grace of God. "It is of the Lord's mercies that we are not consumed;" and that is true of the man who blasphemes God. Where did that man get his breath?—From God. God continues breath to him in his wickedness, in order that the gift may reveal God's goodness and he repent; for it is the goodness of God. He is kind to the evil and the good; he sends rain upon the just and the unjust; that is God.

He [God] giveth to all life, and breath, and all things, and hath made of one blood all nations of men for to dwell on all the face of the earth, that they should seek the Lord, if haply they might feel after him, and find him, though he be not far from every one of us: for in him we live, and move, and have our being; as certain also of your own poets have said, For we are also his offspring. Acts 17:25-28.

What am I doing now?—Moving. How am I able to move?—By the power of God. It is God's power by which I move. Now, as I am moving, making this motion [throwing out the arms], I am not doing any harm. But suppose I get nettled at some one, and I come so close to him that his head should be near where my fist is as I strike out, and I should hit him; would it be a different force which I use?—No; the strength that we use to fight even against God is simply the power of God in us,—Christ's power in the man. The goodness and long-suffering of God is such that he will stay with us, and let his power be so prostituted and turned against him, in hope that we shall be brought to repentance. Here is the glorious truth—in him we move. If we are willing to allow God to use his own power, his own way, then all our movements will be just such as God prompts. Fourteenth verse:—

Forasmuch then as the children are partakers of flesh and blood, he also himself likewise took part of the same; that through death he might destroy him that had the power of death, that is the devil; and deliver them who through fear of death were all their lifetime subject to bondage.

Some one asks, Is the power of God in man when he sins? How are you going to find out? Look to the Word. The Word was made flesh. How many kinds of flesh are there?—One flesh of man. All men are of one flesh. We are all sons of Adam. We are all brethren. We are all relations, and we need not be ashamed to deny the relationship, because the best man is of himself no better than the vilest. Christ is not ashamed. Where does power come from? "Power belongs to God." Is there any other originator of power, or source of power?—No; but there is perverted power. That is rebellion. Suppose the United States should have war with Spain; would that be rebellion?—No. They are two independent nations. But suppose the State of Nebraska should begin war with the United States. O, that is rebellion, because the United States are one power. Men are in rebellion against God because they have turned his power against him. But the fact that we are in rebellion against God, shows that we are his children, fallen, but living only by the power of his life.

I do not want any one to make a purely theoretical thing of this; it is the joy of salvation. It is the power of the gospel to me personally. It is everything to me. It is what gives me the hope of salvation, and courage to work for fallen humanity who are just as bad, some of them, as I was. I never saw any one in the world that I thought was any worse than I was. Here is a man that does not know the Word. He may say, I don't know anything about it. He may say in his heart, How can I find the way? how can I know how to be right? I can't find God. Say to him, Did you make yourself?—No. Do you support yourself, even when you say you are earning your living? Who gives you your strength? Now, there is one thing we need all the time to keep our lives going. It is air. Did you make this air? Where did you get the air you breathe? It is God's air; it is the breath of God.

God put his own breath into man's nostrils, in order that he might live. That is the way we continue to breathe. It is the breath of God that keeps us alive, the Spirit of God in our nostrils. Well, that man must acknowledge what is so patent that he cannot help but acknowledge it; namely, that he did not bring himself into existence, and that he cannot perpetuate his existence for one instant. He is brought face to face with the power of God in him, keeping him alive. It is Christ in fallen man, it is Christ in cursed man, it is Christ with the curse on him, it is Christ crucified. Christ taking fallen, sinful humanity upon him, is Christ crucified. Do not say in your heart, Who will ascend up into heaven to bring Christ down to me, that is to be crucified? No; he is here in the flesh.

"If thou wilt confess with thy mouth the Lord Jesus." What is it to confess him? To confess a thing is not to make it so, but it is to acknowledge that the thing is so. Now the fact that we are to confess is, that Christ is come in the flesh. O, let me read a word here. Rom.1:18–20: "For the wrath of God is revealed from heaven against all ungodliness and unrighteousness of men, who hold down the truth in unrighteousness." What is the truth? Christ says, "I am the truth." Thus the truth that is stated is that "the wrath of

God is revealed from heaven against all ungodliness and unrighteousness of men" who hold back Christ in them. "Because that which may be known of God is manifest in them; for God hath shewed it unto them;" for ever since the creation of the world, the invisible things of God are clearly seen, "being understood by the things that are made."

Look at the trees; we see the power and the divinity of God in the trees and grass, and in every thing that God has made, and see it clearly, too. But I read that text for years, and forgot that I was one of the things that God made. Am I not one of the things of the creation, just as well as a tree? Then what is seen and understood in the things that God has made, even man not excluded?—His eternal power and divinity. So we are without excuse. Now if thou wilt confess with thy mouth the Lord Jesus, that he is in your flesh,—but do not stop with that confession,—"and shalt believe in thy heart that God has raised him from the dead," lifted him up to his own right hand in the heavenly places, "thou shalt be saved." That is Christ crucified, and raised in every man. When he will confess the truth, and believe the truth, then he has Christ in him, crucified and risen, with the resurrection power, to do whatsoever God says. I tell you there is power in the gospel that can lift a man out of the ditch to the throne of God, and I am glad of it.

Who is like unto the Lord our God, who dwelleth on high, who humbleth himself to behold the things that are in heaven, and in the earth! He raiseth up the poor out of the dust, and lifteth the needy out of the dunghill; that he may set him with princes, even with the princes of his people. Ps.113:5–8.

Thank God for that!

"We love him because he first loved us." "And this commandment have we from him, That he who loveth God love his brother also."

Study Number Seven
(Tuesday Afternoon, February 16, 1897)

This question was handed to me as I came in: "In Rom.13:1 (`There is no power but of God'), does the word `power' have the same signification as in other places?" I do not know why it should mean anything different in one place than it does in another. Power is power, and power belongs to God, and there is no other source of power. It does not seem as though it ought to be difficult for people who believe in God to believe that. Power, without any qualification or limitation, belongs to God, that is, it pertains to him; it is his attribute. Suppose we take it that God has power, but he has not all the power there is. If that were so, there would be another God, would there not?

(A voice) That would make it necessary.

Suppose we say he has some power in the universe, and that there is another being in the universe who has some power. Then the question will be, Which is the greater? There will be a controversy in the universe. Now just such a controversy has arisen—Satan has claimed equality with God, and has presumed to dispute the possession of power. But I thank God there is no question about the outcome, or about the facts. Power belongs to God, and therefore we do not need to wait until the end to find out who is going to come out ahead, in order to arrange ourselves on his side. But we know from the Bible and from the Word of God in all nature, that power, absolute and universal, all the power there is, belongs to God. Don't you see that if it were not so, there would be some part of the universe over which God did not have any right to control.

(A voice) Yes.

And if we could find out who those certain ones are that have power that does not belong to God, we would not have any ground whatever to stand on in preaching the gospel to them. They would say, I never received anything from the Lord, and I don't owe him anything.

Do you not see that the question of division of power is simply the question, How many gods are there? There is one God, and only one.

Well it is wonderful to me, every day I live, and the longer I live the more wonderful it is to me, into how small a space, and how simple a truth, all the truth is resolved. Whoever comes to the recognition of this fact, and holds himself to it as all the truth there is in the universe,—God is, and there is no other; and when we see God is, he that cometh to God must believe that he is. That is his name.—I Am. What?—I Am, absolute. When we come face to face with that, it is a wonderful thought. God is. Where?—He is. Go where you will in the universe, and there it can be said, He is. You know it says in the one hundred and thirty-ninth Psalm:—

Whither shall I go from thy spirit? or whither shall I flee from thy presence? If I ascend up into heaven, thou art there [that is about the only space that some people believe that he has]; and if I make my bed in hell, [that is in the depths, the heart of the earth,] behold thou art there. If I take the wings of the morning, and dwell in the uttermost parts of the sea; even there shall thy hand lead me, and thy right hand shall hold me.

Why should any one try to minimize the power of God, or to claim that the power is divided between him and another being? Do you not see that in so doing a man is taking the foundation from under his own feet? What confidence can we have in God if he is not the only supreme, absolute, the only God, the only ruler in the universe? If any one can claim power aside or apart from God, we have no hope.

There is one being who has thought to divide divine honors with the Lord. He has said, "I will be like the Most High," and he has instilled that spirit into mankind from the very beginning, saying, In the day ye eat thereof, ye shall be like God. I believe that was why our first parents cut loose from God. They thought that they could get along without him, therefore they did not need to obey him. It is all involved in that; Satan said, I have power outside of God, I am independent of him. Satan made them believe that God was arbitrary, and was trying to keep them from heaven, so that they would not know, and so he could arrogate all honors to himself. Then they ate so that they might get the power that God had been keeping back from them. But they failed, for power belongs only to God. When they put forth their hand to take that which was to give them power to make them like God, thinking that they could maintain their existence independent of him, in that very day came death. Then they found that there was no power but God, and that the devil had lied to them.

Now, God in his mercy and long-suffering allowed his power to be prostituted, allowed men to use his power, even against him. Why?—Because he is merciful and loving, sending his rain on the evil and the good; his sunshine on the just and the unjust, in order that the goodness of God might reveal the truth, the power that belongs to God.

That lesson that we came to study yesterday in the second chapter of Hebrews, is so important that we must spend time upon that, studying the Scriptures and showing how plainly it is revealed, that God is in Christ, in everything, because God is manifest only in Christ.

And so it makes no difference which term we use in speaking, God, or Christ, it is that power, because Christ is the power and the wisdom of God. Wherever Christ is, there is the power of God. Wherever the power of God is, there is Christ.

So that we may see that we are not wandering from this study in Hebrews, we will read, beginning with these verses:—

But now we see not yet all things put under him. But we see Jesus, who was made a little lower than the angels for the suffering of death, crowned with glory and honor; that he by the grace of God should taste death for every man. For it became him, for whom are all things, and by whom are all things, in bringing many sons unto glory, to make the Captain of their salvation perfect through sufferings. For both he that sanctifieth and they who are sanctified are all of one: for which cause he is not ashamed to call them brethren, saying, I will declare thy name unto my brethren, in the midst of the church will I sing praise unto thee. And again, I will put my trust in him. And again, Behold I and the children which God hath given me. For as much then as the children are partakers of flesh and blood, he also himself likewise took part of the same; that through death he might destroy him that had the power of death, that is, the devil: and deliver them who through fear of death were all their lifetime subject to bondage. For verily he took not on him the nature of angels.

He goes right back to the beginning. Unto the angels hath he not put in subjection the world to come; therefore, since Christ's sacrifice has, so far as we are concerned, to do with this world, he took not on him the nature of angels, but he took on him the seed of Abraham:—

Wherefore in all things it behooved him to be made like unto his brethren, that he might be a merciful and faithful high priest, in things pertaining to God, to make reconciliation for the sins of the people.

What we read yesterday in the tenth chapter of Romans, we will look at again. "The righteousness which is of faith, speaketh on this wise, Say not in thine heart, Who shall ascend into heaven? (that is, to bring Christ down.)" That is, Christ came down voluntarily. He humbled himself, and became obedient unto death, even the death of the cross. "Or, Who shall descend into the deep? (that is, to bring up Christ again from the dead.)" Or, when the gospel is preached through Christ, the word can be said to every soul, Now you do not need to say, Where will I find him? This is just where perhaps nine hundred and ninety-nine thousandths of the preaching of the gospel does not reach the people,—because it fails to make the connection between God and the people. Yes, believe on the Lord. But, what? Where is he? Where may I find the Lord? How can I know about Christ crucified and risen? It does not say that. The Word is Christ. Now do not say, Who came to bring the Word to us, or Christ to us, in order that we might be made righteous to keep the law. No; what saith it?—The Word is in them. It is in thy mouth. Or, in thy mouth, and in thy heart, literally.

What is the word of faith which we preach?—"That if thou shalt confess with thy mouth the Lord Jesus, and shalt believe in thine heart that God hath raised him from the dead, thou shalt be saved." Now, what is the great fact, the great truth, about the Lord Jesus that is to be confessed with the mouth? Why, that the Word was made flesh—that is the thing to be confessed, Confess the Lord Jesus. Why confess Christ?—Because to confess a thing is to say it is so. To confess the Lord Jesus in the flesh, is to confess that Christ is the power of God; and that is to confess that this is not of men at all. This life I have is not my life. It is God's.

It is God's in the most absolute sense. The breath of God, and the Word—these are even in thy mouth. It is the manifestation of God's power. Then when a man confesses that, he simply gives up, he renounces all his assumptions to power, and of right to rule; all ownership of himself that he has claimed to have, he gives up, and he is the Lord's because this life is the life that God has given. It is the breath that God has lent. I am living upon his bounty; not only so, but it is his life within.

Knowing that fact—that Christ, the Lord, the power of God, is in my flesh—now I will believe in my heart that God has raised him from the dead; that is, gives him the victory over the infirmity of the flesh, even over death. Then I have Christ crucified and risen again in the flesh, and when I believe in that Christ risen to the right hand of God, that lifts me up so long as I believe. With the heart man believeth unto righteousness.

Here is a message to God's people; and when you read this you will see that it is not by chance that we are taking up these things today.

Let us turn to the fortieth chapter of Isaiah:—

The voice of him that crieth in the wilderness, Prepare ye the way of the Lord, make straight in the desert a highway for our God. Every valley shall be exalted, and every mountain and hill shall be made low: and the crooked shall be made straight, and the rough places plain: and the glory of the Lord shall be revealed, and all flesh shall see it together: for the mouth of the Lord hath spoken it. Verses 3–5.

Now, what is this voice crying in the wilderness, "Prepare ye the way of the Lord."—The voice was that of John the Baptist. (See John 1:19–23.)

But did John the Baptist finish the message?—No. Read further:—

And the glory of the Lord shall be revealed, and all flesh shall see it together: for the mouth of the Lord hath spoken it. The voice said, Cry. And he said, What shall I cry? All flesh is grass, and all the goodliness thereof is as the flower of the field: the grass withereth, the flower fadeth: because the spirit of the Lord bloweth upon it: surely the people is grass. The grass withereth, the flower fadeth: but the Word of our God shall stand forever. O Zion, that bringest good tidings, get thee up into the high mountain; O Jerusalem that bringest good tidings, lift up thy voice with strength; lift it up, be not afraid; say unto the cities of Judah, Behold your God! Behold, the Lord God will come with strong hand, and his arm shall rule for him: behold, his reward is with him, and his work before him. Verses 5–10.

In the last chapter of the Bible we read: "Behold, I come quickly, and my reward is with me." But here it reads, "Prepare ye the way of the Lord." Then the work of John the Baptist was to prepare for the second coming of Christ; as well as for the first. And that message is to be given today. He is to come and rule with a strong arm; "and his work [is] before him." That is the last message. It must be. The last message is the Lord's coming, and his coming is near. We often speak of the third angel's message going with power, or with a loud voice, "the loud cry." What have we here?—"Lift up thy voice with strength; lift it up, be not afraid." Then this is the loud cry of the third angel's message. This is what we have here in the fortieth chapter of Isaiah. It is the last message going with a loud cry, saying, "Say unto the cities of Judah, Behold your God." Where? says one. I cannot see him; where is he? Get your eyes open then. That is the last message, Behold your God. Where?—In the things which he has made. Now, this is an essential part of the message. We have seen where it points to—the end. That is the Lord's coming with power, and it is the message proclaimed with a mighty voice. What shall I cry? What message shall I give?—"All flesh is grass, and all the goodliness thereof is as the flower of the field: the grass withereth, the flower fadeth: because the spirit of the Lord bloweth upon it: surely the people is grass. The grass withereth, the flower fadeth: but the Word of our God shall stand forever."

What is the message, then,—the last message to be given to the people?—Behold your God; the mighty one. All flesh is grass, but the Word of the Lord abides. In short, man himself is nothing; God is everything. Now take this simple statement: "All flesh is grass." Is that true? We try sometimes to evade that, saying, All flesh is like grass. But "all flesh is grass."

Take the first chapter in Genesis. We have not half begun to learn that chapter. If we knew the first chapter of Genesis thoroughly, there would not be much of the Bible that we could not see through clearly. Let us read in three different places here in this chapter. First, the eleventh verse:—

And God said, Let the earth bring forth grass, the herb yielding seed, and the fruit tree yielding fruit after his kind, whose seed is in itself, upon the earth: and it was so.

From where does the grass come then?—Out of the earth. He said, Let the earth bring it forth, and the earth obeyed. The earth had no power of itself to bring forth grass, but when he put his Word into it, then the grass came; and so it is that grass still grows. The Word abides forever; it still says, Bring forth grass, and the grass grows by the power of that Word. The twenty-fourth verse:—

And God said, Let the earth bring forth the living creature after his kind, cattle and creeping thing and beast of the earth after his kind: and it was so.

The same thing, just the same thing that was said of the grass. Let the earth bring forth the grass, now let the earth bring forth the beast. Grass and beast came from the same place. "And the Lord God formed man out of the dust of the ground." Grass, beast, man, comes from the earth. Man, just like others, is grass. All flesh is grass; it grows out of the ground—by what power?—The power of God. By that power we live. All are of dust, and all return to dust again, Then there is not so much difference between the grass of the field and us. Christ said, "Consider the lilies of the field;" but, there is another lily, for "Israel shall grow as the lily."

Where does man get his support? Where does his life come from? Where does man get his food? There is not anything that man eats that does not come from the ground. The beasts of the field eat the herbs. All flesh is grass. There are many forms of grass, not only the grass we tread upon, but the wheat is one form of grass; herbs are only different forms of grass, and God has given them to man to eat. The trees are of the same nature as grass, so we have creation all as grass; but the Word of God abides.

We may learn lessons from the grass. How often we have gone out just as the grass or the Indian corn was beginning to spring forth, and as we passed along we noticed a big clod of earth detached and rising up. It might weigh several pounds. And then we had the curiosity to look under it; and what did we see?—just a little blade of grass, perhaps a blade of wheat, so tiny and small it had no color to it yet;—just a little white mass of fiber and water; that is all, nothing to it. It was just standing upright, and not only standing upright under that clod of earth, but it was steadily pushing it out of the way, and was just keeping its place and going right along, regardless of this clod. It is safe to say that a blade of grass pushes away a weight ten thousand times its own weight. If a man had as much power according to his size and weight, he could lift a mountain: he could take up Pike's Peak, and throw it off as a lad would a football.

But when you take it out of there, it will not hold itself up. It just yields—it is gone. If you even remove the clod, it cannot stand. That blade of grass is not such a little thing after all, but it is undeniable that there was a wonderful power manifested in that blade of grass. But what was that power?—God's own life, his own personal presence there, doing in the grass just what he designed for the grass; it was God that was working in it, both to will and to do of his own good pleasure.

Not only his power, but his wisdom. How often we have seen a tree sending its roots all off to one side, no roots on the other side at all. Why did it do that?—O, because there was a stream of water over here; but on the other side it was dry and barren. How did that tree know that there was water over there? Not only so, but if a root of the tree in going along on its wonted course to find water, finds an obstruction in the way that it cannot pierce, it will go down under and come up, and go on there. Is that chance? There is no chance about it.

Botanists tells us, and we know it, that each different kind of plant requires a different kind of food. There are little fibers sent out from the roots; these fibers are the mouths by which it takes up its nourishment. These fibers gather around a portion of earth. But those who have observed closely will tell us that these roots will discriminate and go out to find the soil they need for their nourishment. How do they know how to do this? That is what the birds and beasts do. They go where they can find the proper food for their nourishment. Man does the same thing. We have seen the power that was in that blade of grass, and it was the power of God, and that is Christ, But Christ is not only the power of God, but he is the wisdom of God; and so both the power and the wisdom of God are in that blade of grass. The plant acknowledges its helplessness. The plant never assumed to be something it was not made to be. The plant never got out of its place. If we pull it out of its place it is good for nothing. When it was in the place where God put it, it was all right. It is utterly subject to God, and therefore the power of God is manifest in it to bring it to the perfection as grass of the field, with the life of God in it, and that same life of God in it gives it the power to get the water and the nourishment that it needs. When an animal does that thing, we call it instinct. What is it? It is the life which God gives. It is the measure of life which God gives for the beast according to his kind to direct it, and the beast in the perfect state of nature when connected with men, does those things which are necessary for his strength, and health; the wisdom which God has given, is for his perfection as a beast.

But when man does these things, it is not God any more, is it? No, it is because I am so wise, and I have such keen perception. No, no, it is the life of God. Whatever wisdom a man has, the strength he has, comes from Him. "Thus saith the Lord, Let not the wise man glory in his wisdom, neither let the mighty man glory in his might, let not the rich man glory in his riches: but let him that glorieth, glory in this,"—that I am the Lord?—No; "that he understandeth and knoweth me that I am the Lord." In pursuance of this thought, that all flesh is as grass. We are all plants together, with one life in us all. Now we noticed that plant that was in the ground with a clod of earth upon it. It had no power in itself whatever to lift off that clod, but there was a mighty power in it, and it is so that if any man in proportion to the grass had proportionate power in him, he could lift the Alps. Our Saviour said, "If ye had faith as a grain of mustard seed," ye could lift a mountain. Now was that guess work?—All that is faith, absolute dependence upon God. Instead of being frightened or discouraged or disgusted because we are only grass, that is our hope. What God can do with the grass of the field he can do with us if we will have the faith. God will do for us what he does for that.

What life therefore is manifested everywhere in the universe?—The life of Christ. Christ in the flesh crucified and risen, Christ in the flesh crucified in me, because if Christ is crucified some distance from me, even though it be close beside me, it is far away. I cannot make the connection. But when I know that that life which was offered, and which was powerful enough to gain the victory over sin and death, that very same life is in me, and confess it and believe it, everything that that life can do is mine. Take a verse that is familiar to us all: "Then said I, Lo, I come: in the volume of the book it is written of me. I delight to do thy will, O my God, yea, thy law is within my heart." That is to say, thy law is my life, and that is exactly what is in the last verse of the twelfth chapter of John: "And I know that his commandment [that is in man] is life everlasting: whatsoever I speak therefore, even as the Father said unto me, so I speak." And this is life eternal, that we might know the only true God, and the Son whom he has sent. To know him and Christ is eternal life; therefore the law of God is simply life. It is the law of life—the law of the spirit of life in Christ Jesus—which has made us free from the law of sin and death. So the law of God is simply the life of God; it is his life. Then there cannot be anything arbitrary about it. People think of the laws of God as something that he made as an earthly ruler would make laws; that is, God made man, and then he thought, Now, what law would I better make for his guidance that is good for man? But God did not do that way. The law was his life. He put the life into the man as his law, and so long as that man would consent to be absolutely controlled by him, he would be a holy man, a godly man.

We speak of the laws of nature and the laws of God; or, of the natural law, and the moral law. What is the difference between them? Natural law, that is, we see a plant, and it grows in a certain way, and it always grows in the right way; it will grow in the way that God has made it. It lets God live his own life in it. Then what are called natural laws are simply the life of God manifested in the things we see,—the being that is perfect after its kind. It is the same life in the grass, in the vine, in the oak tree. But God made the grass after its kind, and the vine to be another thing after its kind, and the oak tree to be another thing after its kind; and the same life in all brings each to perfection after its kind. And he made man after his kind—to be grass, it is true, dust, but to have the supreme position on earth. And the life of God in the man, if you will yield to it as implicitly as the grass and the trees, will bring him to perfection after his kind, to the perfection that God has designed for him.

Now what would be the case if this grass should begin to assume that it would be an oak tree; it will not be grass, but it will grow into an oak tree, and claim to be something it is not?—Then God's plan is not perfected in it. It resists God's life. It says, I don't want to be this way; I want to be that way, and I will make myself that. And the whole thing is frustrated. So we see that the law is one, and that it is God's life, and it is not an arbitrary arrangement, but God is the author and source of life, and his life works in all his creatures so far as they let him. But now we see not all things put under him. We see a curse; and why?—Because the curse came upon the earth. But first the curse came upon man, and then upon the earth because of man's sin. What was the curse that fell upon man?—Death.

Because of sin, came the curse and death. Death in the absence of life. So death fell upon man because he rejected the life of God. He said, I will be God; I will not be dependent upon him; I will take this thing, this fruit—and you know that was the only thing he could see in the garden. He thought God had deprived him of everything because this one thing was kept back. He thought that all the other was nothing; he thought he must have that in order to live. So he said I will take of this one tree, which will put me in my right, and give me my power, so that I can be independent of God, and I will cast him off. What did he get?—He got the absence of life. God in his mercy did not take man at his word, and let him be utterly separated from him, because, if he had, he would have continued in death. But he continues his life to man in his weak and fallen state. But now he is fallen. We do not see the perfection of life. We see the curse upon the earth, because of man's sin.

Thorns and thistles are simply evidence of weakness, of the diminution of the life-power. The weakness of man, as well as of beasts, is evidence of the reduction of the life-power, that is the absence of Christ. Christ has taken all our weakness upon himself, so that when we accept him and know him, and have a knowledge of him, then we are made new creatures: "If any man be in Christ, he is a new creature." Instead of bringing forth thorns and thistles and briers to be rejected, he brings forth fruit unto everlasting life, to the glory of God.

"Build a little fence of trust around today;

Fill it in with living deeds and therein stay.

Look not through the sheltering bars upon tomorrow;

God will help thee bear what comes of joy or sorrow."

Study Number Eight
(Wednesday Afternoon, February 17, 1897)

We are studying God, the power of God. What words in the second chapter of Hebrews have brought this subject before our minds?—"We see Jesus." That covers the whole thing. And in what capacity is he presented there for us to see?—"A little lower than the angels." He is as man. Under what circumstances are we directed to look at him? under what circumstances is he set forth?

(Answered by the congregation) "Crowned with glory and honor."

But before that, what?

In death, crucified. The suffering of death is first. He tasted death for every man, so that in these words, "We see Jesus," we are to see him in the capacity of man. But under what circumstances are we to see Jesus tasting death for every man? When we preach Christ, as Paul says, "We preach Christ crucified." But that expression, "Christ crucified," embraces the resurrection as well; and the resurrection embraces "crowned with glory and honor."

Yesterday we went to the fortieth chapter of Isaiah, and in that chapter we found the message which says, "Prepare ye the way of the Lord"—"All flesh is grass." But that is not all, because if that were all, it would leave us nowhere. There is another part of it—The Word of the Lord endures forever. And the message then is summed up thus: "Say unto the cities of Judah, Behold your God." And thus: "We see Jesus;" "Say unto the cities of Judah, Behold your God."

The lesson therefore that we are to learn now—and I do not see any use of our going further along in this book at present until we can grasp that lesson, or until we can learn to obey this injunction—is, "Behold your God." Let us look at the fortieth chapter of Isaiah a few moments further:—

The glory of the Lord shall be revealed, and all flesh shall see it together: for the mouth of the Lord hath spoken it. The voice said, Cry. And he said, What shall I cry? All flesh is grass, and all the goodliness thereof is as the flower of the field: the grass withereth, the flower fadeth: because the Spirit of the Lord bloweth upon it: surely the people is grass. The grass withereth, the flower fadeth; but the word of our God shall stand forever. O Zion, that bringest good tidings, get thee up into the high mountain; O Jerusalem, that bringest good tidings, lift up thy voice with strength; lift it up, be not afraid; say unto the cities of Judah, Behold your God! Behold, the Lord will come with strong hand, and his arm shall rule for him: behold, his reward is with him, and his work before him.

Here is a message that the one who proclaims it need not be afraid to declare: "Lift up thy voice with strength; lift it up, be not afraid; say unto the cities of Judah, Behold your God." This last message, then, is to point out God to the people so that they can see him.

It will not be necessary for anybody to point out the Lord when he comes, and tell people to see him. They will see him without his being pointed out. "Every eye shall see him." It will not be necessary then for you to call some one's attention, and say, Behold your God, because they who know the Lord will be looking for him, and they will know him. It will not be of any use then to say to sinners, "Behold your God," for it will be too late. Therefore this message, "Behold your God," is to be proclaimed before the Lord comes; so that when he does come, his people will know him, and they will say, "Lo, this is our God, we have waited for him." It would not be right to say to those who knew not God, "Behold your God," for he is not then their God. Every man in the world has made gods to himself, has served gods of his own, but the Lord knows that we are ignorant, and he has compassion upon us even though we have said in our hearts, We do not want the Lord. We have said by our actions, We do not care to have him over us. Our works have denied him, but God does not take us at our word. He says, They are poor, ignorant children. They do not know what they are talking about. The Son says, I will go and declare thy name unto my brethren. "And they that know thy name will put their trust in thee; for thou, Lord, hast not forsaken them that seek thee." Ps.9:10. Every one who knows the Lord must trust him, must love him, because he is trustworthy and lovable.

Now as the message to be proclaimed for these last days is to prepare a people for the Lord when he shall be revealed, and every eye shall see him, we know it will be right to say, Behold the Lord. The work of those who profess to give the message or accept the message is to say to the world, Behold your God, and to give the message to all. Has the Lord cast off all the poor, ignorant weak people in the world—the heathen—whether in this or some other country?—No, he loves them and counts them still his children. You know the story in the fifteenth chapter of Luke. The prodigal son took his father's goods, and went off and wasted them. The father did not cast him off; but that he loved him and longed for his return is shown by the fact that when he saw him afar off he ran to meet him, and said, "This my son was dead, and is alive again. He was lost and is found." So all the time he was gone he had never forgotten him; he still regarded him as one of his children, and longed for him to come back. Now this is the way the Lord looks at all the people on the earth. He calls them his children, and he longs for them to return and to learn of him.

The devil has deceived the world. He has borne false witness against God, and he has made all, to a greater or less extent, believe that God is unjust and overbearing, and that he does not concern himself particularly with the affairs of men. Now we are to go to the world and say to them, Behold your God. But before we can do that, it will be necessary that we ourselves know him. Suppose I go out with that message, and say, Behold your God, and some one asks, Where is he? but I do not see him, what shall I do? We must be able to show God. Where can we see and learn of God?—In the things that he has made. His eternal power and divinity are seen in the works of his hands. So when we learn to see him in his works, then we can say to the people, Behold your God.

But God is revealed in Christ. Because all these things that were made, were made by Christ the Word. Very well, but Christ as he is present before the world, is presented as Christ crucified and raised again. He is the One of whom we are to say, This is our God. We must cause the people to see him crucified for them, and risen again for their justification. Just as we have read in Rom.10:6–9. It does not say, Who shall go up into the heavens, to bring Christ down to us that we may see him; it does not say, Who shall go into the deep to bring Christ up from the deep, that we may have the benefit of his sacrifice; but, The Word, Christ, the Word of faith which we preach, is nigh thee.

Have we not an illustration of that in the sermon of Paul before the Athenians? They were groping after God, feeling after him in their ignorance. He said, God is not worshiped with man's hands. He is not far from every one of us. Did he mean by that that he was a little way off?—No; in him we live, and move, and have our being. Then he is so near that he is identified with us. God, the Lord, the Word that was made flesh for us, has identified himself with man so closely that the bonds can never be broken, never be dissolved; he is one with human flesh, and will be through all eternity.

Now I say that when we can see that this is a living reality to us, there is courage and strength for us. Why, here I am, a sinner myself. I want to put my sins on the Lord, I want to be led of him; not only the sins that I have committed, but this sinful disposition. How am I going to do it?—"Cast all your care upon him." How are we going to cast upon him all our care? This is a practical question.

How many actually know how to cast their cares upon the Lord? Shall I try to gather them all up in a bundle, and throw it on the Lord?—No, we cannot do that. If we remember the first words that we learned in the book of Hebrews, we have it—"upholding all things by the word of his power." He bears all things. All things are included. Sin is included; yes, he bears our sins; he bears all the sorrow and infirmities of the world. But suppose I do not believe that fact,—and there are many who do not,—does that make any difference? Now, there is the statement: He bears all things by the word of his power. But if I do not believe that, will that make any difference with the fact? God is true, though every man is a liar. Who is the liar?—He is a liar who does not believe the Word of God. That is the liar always, because whosoever does not believe God, makes him a liar; that is, whosoever does not believe the Word of God, virtually says, God is a liar. When any one says, God is a liar, what is he doing?—He himself is lying. And who is it that says, God is a liar?—Every one that does not believe.

Let us see. There is a word here in the first epistle of John, second chapter, and twenty-first verse. It will come right in here very well: "Who is a liar, but he that denieth that Jesus is the Christ?" Well, now, it is easy enough to say that Jesus Christ is the Son of God; but it is one thing to say it, and another thing to know it, to believe it. What is meant by that, that he is the Christ?—The Anointed, the Saviour. What is his work as the Christ?—It is to save, to come into personal touch with the individual, to bear sins; yes, to bear our sins. How many sins does Christ bear?—The sins of all. You have that in the first part of the second chapter: "He is the propitiation for our sins,"—and then we forget the rest of the verse, very likely,—"and not for ours only, but also for the sins of the whole world." John said, "Behold the Lamb of God, which taketh away the sin of the world," literally, "that beareth the sins [plural] of the world." What brought death?—Sin. He tasted death for every man. Therefore, how many sins did he have upon him?—The sins of every man.

Now we are coming to the same thing again. He bears the sins of every man. That is a fact. Now, I hope it is a fact that we have believed that so much that we have been content that he should bear them, and not we. Does it lessen the load in the least if we continue to bear them all?—No, he bears them anyhow. If we deny this, there is no faith in Christ at all, because there is the simple statement, He was manifested to take away our sins. He takes them away by bearing them away. He hears them, and takes them away. If we do not consent that he shall bear them, if we are not willing to acknowledge that he does bear them, but allow them to be upon ourselves, then, of course, we make him a liar, and that makes us liars, and we get no practical benefit of the arrangement.

But now he bears the sins of the world. Take ourselves, even before we were converted; did he bear our sins then.—Yes. Well, did you ever commit a sin, or have a sin or a sinful habit that was somewhere off away from you? If that sin had even been one foot away from you, if there was a clear space between you and the sin, you could have gotten along pretty well. The trouble was the sin was right in you all the time. And because we were sinful, there was sin in us, and we ourselves were sin. We had the burden of it; but all the time what was true of Christ?—He was bearing our sins. Where was he, then?—In us; he was living in us—not in a general way. Christ is not in us in a general way, but personally and individually.

We must find out for ourselves whether we believe the simplest things which the gospel presents. Christ bears the sins of the world, and he has done so from the beginning. You have heard the story often about the man who was going along the road with a bag of corn on his shoulder, and a neighbor came along with a wagon, and asked him to come and ride. So he got up and sat in the seat behind; and pretty soon the driver looked around and saw the man with the bag of corn still on his shoulder, and he said, Why don't you lay that down?—O, it is too much for the horse. It is enough for him to carry me without my load.

Now, if we carry our sins, does that lessen the load from the Lord?—No; he still carries them. This is no speculation. We are trying to come to practical facts, and if we believe them, and do not hold them off, we will find all the good there is in them. He bears the sins of the world. But now there are many people who never become rid of their sins. There may be some here. If there is one here who has never known what it is to get rid of his sins, then I hope this lesson will help him to see clearly and understand how to let the sin go, and get rid of it; because I have no message whatever to the people to say in a general way, Come to the Lord and accept him as your Saviour, and let your sins be on him, and he will save you. It is easy to say that, but people do not understand it. Where is he, that I should come to him? Where can I find him? They do not see that. Poor people by the thousands, who are honest, and earnest, and eager to get rid of sin and to live righteous lives, accept him; they think if they will believe something, why the Lord will bless them—and he does. The Lord in his infinite mercy takes the slightest whisper, the slightest impulse, even the thought that is afar off, and meets it, and works on account of it. But yet we know—I know, and you know from your own experience—that there are many people who confess Christ, profess to be Christians, who have no clearly defined idea what it is to come to the Lord, to find the Lord, and to know him, and to be personally acquainted with him.

Now what we want is to stop trifling. If the Lord is so near, and to be found, we want to find him; and he says: Seek ye the Lord while he is near. While he may be found, call upon him. While he is near, O, so near that you do not have to go across the room; you do not have to go anywhere at all but here; he is within you. He was so near me all those years that I did not know anything about him, and he was bearing my sin. Why?—Because the Lord Jesus is in everything that he has made. He upholds all things, because he is in them. He is cohesion even to inanimate nature. It is the personal, powerful presence of God that keeps the mountains together, and the stones from crumbling to pieces; because God is there with his personal power. And we saw yesterday about the grass, and the trees, and the rootlets,—that they take up the nourishment that is adapted to them, and leave to one side that which is not fitted for them. That fine discrimination which takes what is necessary for them, and leaves the other aside, we saw was nothing but the power of God doing for them just what we say is instinct in the animals; and when it comes to man, we call it reason. That is God's personal presence. Now if we acknowledge that he is in us, that we are as grass and plants, and acknowledge that as truly as the grass itself does, then this power of God will lead us to make just the same right choice as does the grass, the rootlet, and the tree, in choosing that which is necessary for them.

"But of him are ye in Christ Jesus, who of God is made unto us wisdom and righteousness." But the trouble is, people will not acknowledge this. They are not willing to acknowledge that they have no power, and so reason that they do not need the Lord, and do not let the Lord take possession of them. In the first chapter of Romans, after stating that that which may be known of God, his eternal power and divinity, is manifested since the creation of the world in the things which he has made, we have this:—

So that they are without excuse: because that, when they knew God, they glorified him not as God, neither were thankful; but became vain in their imagination, and their foolish heart was darkened. Professing themselves to be wise, they became fools, and changed the glory of the incorruptible God into an image made like to corruptible man, and to birds, and four-footed beasts, and creeping things.

They (the heathen, the people) became vain in their reasonings, and their fleshly heart was darkened. And so we read in 2Cor.10:4,5,—

(For the weapons of our warfare are not carnal, but mighty through God to the pulling down of strong holds;) casting down imaginations, and every high thing that exalteth itself against the knowledge of God, and bringing into captivity every thought to the obedience of Christ.

This means that what we deify as human reason, is simply folly. "Professing themselves to be wise, they became fools." So that deified human reasoning, apart from the Lord, is simply folly. If men would reason rightly, they must leave themselves in the hands of God, whose power works in them, for him to be their reasoning: for he chooses for them. The word "heretic" means one who chooses for himself. Now that does not mean that the man who does not choose the thing which I say, is a heretic,—that the man who does not choose for himself aside from the church, is a heretic. No; the whole church may be heretics, yet they may be orthodox according to the creed. The man is a heretic who chooses for himself, instead of letting God choose. When we believe that all flesh is grass, we simply allow God in us to choose for us as he chooses in the rootlet and the plant, to select that thing which is necessary. The rootlet will go a long distance in search of what it needs, and will find it every time. It will go a long distance to find moisture, and leave the dry place alone. It is passive in the hands of the Lord, and the Lord chooses for it, and it is simply right.

We are to learn this truth, to behold God in the things he has made. Thus we are to behold God in us. In the beginning was the Word, and the Word was with God, and the Word was God, and the Word was made flesh. Then if we believe the Word, we must believe that the Word is flesh. And that truth which, accepted, will lift sinners out of sin, and put them up on high, is a recognition of the simple fact that God is in them; that he is their life, he is their strength; that nothing is apart from God.

Thou hast bought me no sweet cane with money, neither hast thou filled me with the fat of thy sacrifices; but thou hast made me to serve with thy sins, thou hast wearied me with thine iniquities. Isaiah 43:24.

It fills me with shame and regret, and at the same time, with a most wonderful love for the Lord, to think that in all the sins I have been committing all those years, I was making the Lord bear them: that I was worrying him with them. Because he does not love sin. It is distasteful to him; it is disgusting to him; and yet he allowed his life to bear these sins, and was worrying with them. But it should fill everybody with love to think of his long-suffering, that in order to deliver us from these sins, he is willing to stay with us year after year, with these things that we are piling upon him, and still remain there, waiting and waiting for us to recognize that fact that he is here, so that we will let him bear them, and we be freed from them. Now take the fourth chapter of Ephesians. We will begin with the fourth verse:—

There is one body, and one Spirit, even as ye are called in one hope of your calling: one Lord, one faith, one baptism, one God and Father of all, who is above all, and through all, and in you all.

The best Greek translation, if I remember correctly, leaves that word "you" out, and reads, "Who is above all, and through all, and in all." Suppose we take it as it reads, "Who is above all, and through all, and in you all." There is not half of you here that believe it even that way because we have that miserable Pharisaic idea, that God is in us as soon as we are good enough for him to come into us,—God is in us because we are not like those sinners. Is that not the Pharisaical prayer?—Yes. As Christians, we believe that Christ comes to dwell in us, and yet we think of it as in a sort of general way afar off. But here he is above all, and through all, and in you all. Is it true?—Yes; the spirit of God standing here and speaking to this congregation says, "And in you all." He is not in us all because we are good, because we can thank God that we are not as this poor sinner. He is above all, and through and in all.

But unto every one of us is given grace according to the measure of the gift of Christ. Wherefore he saith, When he ascended up on high, he led captivity captive, and gave gifts unto men. (Now that he ascended, what is

58 • Studies in the Book of Hebrews

it but that he also descended first into the lower parts of the earth? He that descended is the same also that ascended up far above all heavens, that he might fill all things.) Verses 7–10.

We here have the death and resurrection of Christ brought to view. The same thing that we have before us all the time. Now while it is a fact that God, yea, the Lord Jesus Christ, is in all things, he does not fill all things yet, because men are fighting against, and holding down, and opposing the truth. But the purpose of God, in the crucifixion and the ascension, is that he might fill all things as in the beginning, absolutely fill them. But because of man's sin, God does not absolutely fill from creation, and the fullness of God is not seen. In the beginning, the absolute perfection of God was seen in everything he had made. Now it is not. But God's purpose is that they shall be restored, and he ascended on high so that he might fill everything. Now going back to the third chapter:—

For this cause I bow my knees unto the Father of our Lord Jesus Christ,…that Christ may dwell in your hearts.

Thus we see that Christ may dwell in our hearts. But in the tenth of Romans the words are addressed to those who do not know the Lord, but who are groping about, and asking, Where shall we find him? "The Word is nigh thee, even in thy mouth and in thy heart." Then why did the Spirit, through the apostle Paul, pray that Christ may dwell in the heart? When speaking to sinners, he says, The Word, Christ, is in thy heart. But Paul prays that Christ may dwell in your hearts *by faith*. There is a difference, and that is a great difference. Before, Christ was in my heart, and I did not know it. Christ was in my flesh, he was my life, in him I moved and had my being. It was his power that caused my blood to circulate; his life was all that I had, but I did not know it, I did not care anything about it. But do you not see that as soon as a man recognizes that fact, believes that fact, and lives in daily conscious recognition of that fact that Christ is in him, that Christ is his life, that he has no life or power whatever but the life and power of Christ, it makes a vast difference with that man's life? He will say, O, I do not belong to myself at all; I thought I had a right to do as I please, but I have not; this is not my power or strength.

God is the only one who has a right to control a man. And when Christ dwells in the heart by faith, then the petition will be fulfilled: "That ye, being rooted and grounded in love, may be able to comprehend with all saints what is the breadth, the length, and depth, and height, and to know the love of Christ, which passeth knowledge, that ye might be filled with all the fullness of God." Instead of repressing him, with unrighteousness, and simply allowing him to give us enough of his life to sustain our daily physical lives, we will take enough of his life to keep us going, and allow him to fill us with all his fullness. There is a vast difference. Crucified and risen in the flesh, in every man's flesh, I carry to the people that message, Behold your God, crucified and risen, not far from you, but in your mouth and heart; believe that he is your life, that he was crucified and has risen to deliver you from death and sin. When we recognize that, then he will fill us. If we do not, then the Scripture is fulfilled, "Man that is in honor, and understandeth not, is like the beasts that perish."

But God has made man for a higher position than that of the beasts. If we simply allow him to live in us this physical life, we get no more from him than the beasts get. But God did not make us to be beasts; he made man for his own companionship. He made men to be like him, because they are like him. We are his offspring, his children, made to be associates, friends, and to be associated with him,—I do not know how to express it so that you will not get a wrong idea,—but it is to be on terms of equality; and although he is so far above us, he does not make us feel that he is coming down or condescending to talk with us; and when we get into heaven, although we may recognize to all eternity that he is infinitely beyond every other being in the universe, we will feel no more restraint in coming into his presence than we would to go into the presence of our earthly parents. We will be as a child coming to its father, without any reserve or restraint. That is what he made us for.

Now if you are content that he should give us no more of his life than he gives to the beasts, then our reasoning faculties become like those of the beasts. Those men who, when they knew God, glorified him not as God, did not honor him, but became vain in their reasonings, and became fools, and changed the glory of the incorruptible God into an image made like unto corruptible man—they forgot God, and they worshiped the idols of their own hands. And the one hundred and nineteenth Psalm says of these idols and these men, "They that make them are like unto them." So that when these men became vain in their own reasoning, they became like the gods they worshiped. It has been a wonderful help to me to think that there is not a thing that touches humanity—there is not a thing that touches me, there is not anything that I feel, that oppresses me, that hurts me, or causes me pain, physical pain, or any other kind of pain,—there is nothing of which I am conscious, or that affects my system that I am unconscious of, but that it touches the Lord Jesus Christ. If I am sick, every pain that racks my body touches the Lord, and he feels it, because if I were not alive, I could not feel it. It is my sensitiveness, it is my sensibility, my nerves, the life that is in me, that feels that pain. He is my life. He feels it. There is something in this that can lift a man up, and enable him who is weak to become strong. As Paul says, "When I am weak, then am I strong." The sin that I have committed, he felt it more than I did, because I enjoyed it, and he did not. I loved the sin, but he did not love it; it was disgusting to him, but he felt it all. Then I say, Lord, I have done this thing; if you will bear this thing, and you do bear it, just take it. Let it drop on him; he will carry it. He came in the flesh in the person of Jesus of Nazareth, to show us how perfectly in the flesh he could resist sin.

Now it does not mean anything in this world to me, or to anybody else, to look at him, and see *how* he does this, if he does not do it in me. Suppose we look to him for an example; but if Christ is simply an example for us to look at, and we see Jesus of Nazareth, how good he was, how kind he was, how wise he was,—if that were all, I would have no hope. It would be only discouragement; but when he says, Behold your God, where are we to behold him, afar off?—No, right here.

One Being from the beginning to the end allowed God to perfectly fill him. That is the reason why he was so prudent, and did just the right thing, and thought the right thing. He always knew when to answer questions, and when not to say anything. He was just right because God filled him, and that is an illustration of just what he can do. Now, he says that same power is in my flesh. "The Word is in thee, even in thy heart." All right. I have seen what he can do. Now, I will simply believe, and let him do that in me; and then Christ dwells in my heart by faith—and faith is the taking and appropriating of the thing; it is not professing to believe today, and doubting tomorrow. The just shall live by faith. We would not live very long if we breathed today and stopped breathing tomorrow.

Study Number Nine
(Thursday Afternoon, February 18, 1897)

That same lesson that we had before us yesterday and the day before we still have: "We see Jesus," or the message, "Behold your God;" and we need to continue it until we do see him. We will read in the second chapter of Hebrews so that we may have this portion of the Scriptures fresh in our minds, and simply branch out to other scriptures to see more clearly the facts.

Now, I take it that all here reverence the Word of God, so that whenever the Word comes to us there is nothing to do but to accept it. But accepting it is not simply nodding one's head and saying, "That is so." That is not accepting it. A person would starve to death accepting food in that way. If one brings me food and puts it on the table, and I say, "Thank you. I believe that is good food. It looks good. It seems to be the finest kind of food. I thank you,"—I would starve to death if I never did anything more. That is not accepting it.

Now, the Word of God does not come to us to be looked at, admired, or wondered at; much less, of course, to be discussed and dissected; but the Word of God is life, and it comes to us to be life to us, and we accept it only when we let the life develop to its fullest extent, so that we may have through that life all that God designs for us.

We read the scripture, We see Jesus, who for a little while was made lower than the angels, because of the suffering of death, crowned with glory and honor; that he by the grace of God should taste death for every man. Here we have the whole story of the gospel,—the Word made flesh, crucified, and risen in the flesh. That is the thing. Christ crucified and risen again in the flesh. That is clearly brought to view in that verse. There is no doubt about that.

We all agree that in this we clearly see Christ crucified and risen in the flesh, because we see him a little lower than the angels, that is, as man. That is the Word made flesh. We see him tasting death for every man. That is the crucifixion. We see him crowned with glory and honor. That is the resurrection, the raising up to the right hand of God. He tasted death for every man. Then for how many did he receive the life again?—For every man.

"For it became him, for whom are all things, and by whom are all things, in bringing many sons unto glory, to make the Captain of their salvation perfect through sufferings. For both he that sanctifieth and they who are sanctified are all of one: for which cause he is not ashamed to call them brethren."

He is not ashamed to call who brethren?—All he died for. What is the proof that he was not ashamed to call some persons brethren?—Saying, "I will declare thy name unto my brethren;" and the fact that he says, "I will declare thy name unto my brethren," shows these brethren to be in what condition?—Ignorant of his name. They do not know God's name. So Christ in heaven, looking down upon all the poor, debased, oppressed people on earth, who knew not God's name, called them brethren: and in his love and pity he said to the Father, "I will declare thy name unto" them.

"In the midst of the church will I sing praise unto thee. And again, I will put my trust in him. And again, Behold I and the children which God hath given me. Forasmuch then, as the children are partakers of flesh and blood, he also himself likewise took part of the same."

What for?—"That through death he might destroy him that had the power of death." It is not enough for him to destroy death. He must destroy him that had the power of death, that is, the devil. And what else?—"Deliver them who through fear of death were all their lifetime subject to bondage." A bondage of fear then.

Let us turn to the eighth chapter of Romans, and the tenth verse and onward:—

And if Christ be in you, the body is dead because of sin; but the Spirit is life because of righteousness. But if the Spirit of him who raised up Jesus from the dead dwell in you, he that raised up Christ from the dead shall also quicken your mortal bodies by his Spirit that dwelleth in you. Therefore, brethren, we are debtors, not to the flesh, to live after the flesh. For if ye live after the flesh, ye shall die: but if ye through the Spirit do mortify the deeds of the body, ye shall live. For as many as are led by the Spirit of God, they are the sons of God. For ye have not received the spirit [what spirit?] of bondage again to fear; but ye have received the Spirit of adoption, whereby we cry, Abba, Father. The Spirit itself beareth witness with our spirit, that we are the children of God; and if children, then heirs; heirs of God, and joint heirs with Christ.

We are heirs. Mark, there are two different propositions—"Heirs of God, and joint heirs *with* Christ." What is the difference of heirship with those who are joint heirs?—No difference. Now there is one of the most glorious lessons in this that the Lord ever told me. Children and heirs of God! I do not know how many have read that as simply meaning that we inherit God's property. But the text says that we are heirs of God himself. Most of us perhaps have had poor parents; they could not leave us any property at all; but in spite of that, did not they leave us an inheritance? What is the principal thing, the chief thing that we inherit from our fathers?

(Voice.) A name.

Well, the mere title of course is nothing. It is the characteristics, the tendencies, the turn of mind,—that is what we inherit; so that every person in this world has an inheritance from his parents. We have read already in the first chapter of Hebrews, that Christ, the only-begotten Son, has by inheritance a better name than the angels, a shining forth of his glory, and we are joint heirs with Christ. O, we are coming here to the thing, if you will just hold your eyes upon it. That shows us a wonderful possibility. Heirs of God! You remember there is a Psalm which says, "The Lord is the portion of my inheritance." I inherit *him* through the same Spirit of God. Through the eternal, divine Spirit we are made heirs, heirs of God. Then what does this mean? Inherit the characteristic of God? Is that too strong?

(A voice) That is just what it is.

I cannot explain it, because I cannot understand the Spirit of God. I cannot understand God's own existence; but here we have the statement, we are heirs of God, and joint heirs with Christ. Then whatever Christ receives from the Father, that also, when we accept his Spirit, we inherit in him. Therefore whatever characteristics, whatever disposition, whatever thing the Son inherits from the Father, we as joint heirs, heirs of God himself, inherit in him.

It is a mystery, but yet it is a fact that we have all received certain dispositions and tendencies from our parents. This inheritance is seen outwardly in the color of the hair and eyes, in the features, and in our movements and actions. These are our earthly birthright. Now just as we receive these earthly things from our parents, even so from our heavenly Father through the Spirit we receive his characteristics. That is our heavenly birthright.

We get this lesson in the fifth chapter of Romans: "For as by one man's disobedience [what was the result?] many were made sinners." By whose sin were many made sinners?—Adam's. Then we come into the world sinful, don't we? The inheritance we get from our parents,—their characteristics, their tendencies, their evil traits,—you can see in any child. You can see the father in the child again, and all the evils that his parents committed, not only father and mother, but grandfather and grandmother for generations back. All the evil that they did for generations stamped that impress upon them, and that evil has stamped its impress upon us. We need not argue that. We know it. We all recognize that fact, because it has been discouraging, I doubt not, to many of us; and we have often taken it perhaps as an excuse for a failing, saying, "I inherited it." We say, "I cannot change this, because it is a part of my nature. I inherited it from my father or my grandfather." Take the tendency to drink. It is handed down through generations. It comes often from generations back, but it surely shows itself. Now these things are not fictitious: they are ourselves, aren't they? They are a part of our being,—they make us what we are: and *we* cannot change that. We know that we do not have to try to do these evils. They come out spontaneously.

Now take the whole verse. We have no difficulty with the first part, and if we accept the conclusion, we shall be happy:—

For as by one man's disobedience many were made sinners, so by the obedience of one shall many be made righteous. Verse 19.

How is it that by the disobedience of one we have been made sinners?—We have inherited it. And now, by the offer of one in the flesh, we are to be made righteous in the same way. We have the contrast. Just as we came to be poor, fallen, sinful creatures, even so we shall be made righteous. What is righteousness?—Doing right. Then many shall do right; that is clear. And how will many do right?—By the obedience of One. Well, then, if I am made righteous by his obedience, if I do right by his obedience, where does he obey?—In me. What am I doing?—Letting him, submitting to the righteousness of God. Now there was read here the other day a few words from a testimony, and I will call attention to one sentence, which is as follows:—

I have the Word of the Lord plain and decisive that all who see the necessity of organization must themselves become an example by being organized.

What now is the first thing for us to consider? We have nothing to do with what others do, or with general organization, but the only thing that concerns us is our own individual organization.

How are we going to be organized? How is it going to take place? Are we going to do it? Shall I organize myself?—No. It is that same figure that we have already had. I am a living organization, am I not? Is not this body organized?—Yes; the various organs of my body are working together in perfect harmony, and every part is working. That is organization. They are working together perfectly, without any friction, without any lack of harmony, all agreed. What did I do to get myself organized in this way?—I was born so. Then how am I going to get that organization which the Lord wants me to have?—Be born again: become now, not an heir of my earthly ancestors, but an heir of God. That is clear. Is it clear to you? Now, which would we rather have while here studying,—which would you, as a company, rather have, an hour every day spent here in just a pleasant lesson (I do not say that you would get that if I conducted the class), or that as a result of the Bible study we should be organized, made free? Let us see how many there are here who believe that the Lord designs them to be different from what they are, and has something higher and better for them than they have ever received from him, namely, his fullness; who believe that there is a lack; who believe that there is that for us that we have not, the lack of which hinders us in our daily living, and in our work as we may be connected with the cause. Now let us see an expression. How many think that this is so? How many know that this is so? (The larger part of the congregation raised their hands.)

It seems to be quite general. Why is it so?—Because we are not organized. And what are we going to do to get that organization? How are we going to get it?—By yielding to the Lord. How long do we suppose the Lord wants us to wait for that? In other words, is there a point of time in the future that God has fixed when all these blessings, and the fullness of the blessing, will come upon us, so that we must not expect it yet? What time does the Lord give to man?—Today: now is the accepted time. We shall come across that later, as we study the next chapter of Hebrews. The Spirit says, today, *"Today*, if ye will hear his voice, harden not your hearts." "Take heed, brethren, lest there be in any of you an evil heart of unbelief." Notice, it does not say, an evil heart of stealing; an evil heart of fighting, an evil heart of blasphemy, but an evil heart of unbelief. "But exhort one another daily, while it is called today." One day comes after another, but each day as it comes is "today," and that is the only time God has given. The glorious fact, therefore, is that even this very day, if we are willing really to hear the voice of the Lord, we may as individuals be organized on the Lord's perfect plan. We read in the sixty-first of Isaiah:—

The Spirit of the Lord God is upon me; because the Lord hath anointed me to preach good tidings unto the meek; he hath sent me to bind up the brokenhearted, to proclaim liberty to the captives, and the opening of the prison to them that are bound.

Now the Lord speaks that word "liberty," and when the Lord says a thing, what is there?—The thing itself. The Lord says to all captives, "Liberty." Then what has everybody?—Liberty. The chains are broken, and there is nobody that need sit in bondage, because liberty has been given him. Everybody that sits in bondage is, therefore, a willing slave, a willing captive. Nobody need be bound. That is good. The Lord has spoiled principalities and powers; yes, has disarmed them, triumphed over them. He has entered into the strong man's house, and bound him, and spoiled his goods, taken away his armor in which he trusted. Then, when Christ in us obeys,—mark, when Christ *in us* obeys,—how much power has the devil against us?—None. When we allow Christ to fill us through the Spirit, so that we are filled with all the fullness of God, then we have power "over all the power of the enemy." What is our part?—Submission.

Now, that same work of submission is enough for you and me all the rest of our lives. To submit, to give up, and to keep giving up, or rather, to keep *given up*, as new experiences arise, is all we have to do; and it will occupy all our time. There is work enough for us, then, to hold still, and let the Lord fill us with his Spirit, and work us. That does not mean laziness; it is passive activity, if you please; it means being just as active as the Lord himself was; because Christ himself living in us will be just the same as he was when he was here on the earth.

So work. O, there is work enough for us to do. "This is the work of God that ye believe," and believing is receiving: "For as many as received him, to them gave he power to become the sons of God, *even to them that believe* on his name." So that believing Christ is receiving him. Well, we will go further:—

To proclaim the acceptable year of the Lord, and the day of vengeance of our God; to comfort all that mourn: to appoint unto them that mourn in Zion, to give unto them beauty for ashes, the oil of joy for mourning, the garment of praise for the spirit of heaviness; that they might be called trees of righteousness, the planting of the Lord, that he might be glorified.

The Spirit of God is poured out upon all flesh just as freely as the air we breathe; but just as people shut the air out of their houses, just so they shut out the Spirit of God. Every man in the world may be filled with the Spirit. The Spirit of God is poured out upon all flesh just as freely, and without measure, for every one. God wishes us to be filled with the Spirit, as our lungs are filled with air. This reference to the air reminds me of the creation of the first perfect man. God made him of dust. And what did he breathe into his nostrils?—The breath of life. Just simply breath. His own breath he breathed into him, did he?—Yes. But what was that breath?—Life. God breathed his breath into man, and man went on breathing. Breathing what?—The breath of life. What was that breath of life,—what do we breathe?

(A voice) Air.

What is air, then?—It is God's breath. If we knew this not only physically, but spiritually, we should be much more alive than we are. Read in Ex.14:21, of the time when the children of Israel were at the Red Sea:—

And Moses stretched out his hand over the sea; and the Lord caused the sea to go back by a strong east wind all that night, and made the sea dry land, and the waters were divided.

Moses stretched out his hand over the sea, and what was the result?—The Lord caused the sea to go back by a strong east wind all that night, and made the sea dry land, and the waters were divided. Now what a wonderful change there was by a little shifting of the wind. The wind shifted so strongly that night that a thing happened that never happened before nor since. But let us read the inspired words of Moses the next day: "With the blast of thy nostrils the waters were gathered together, the floods stood upright as an heap." Ex.15:8. So then the air or wind is the breath of God's nostrils. That breath God breathes into us day by day, every minute, yea, many times a minute,—his own life. Very good. When God made that first man, and breathed into his nostrils the breath of life, what kind of man was he?—A living man. Yes, but as to his character?

(A voice) Good.

The Lord God saw everything that he had made, including man, and behold, it was very good. The life that God breathed into man was God, and so long as man continued to acknowledge that his life, his breath, came from God, he remained good. Suppose that at every breath we acknowledged him, then what kind of beings would we be?—Good. We would not say that we were good, but the Lord himself would say that. We can never say of ourselves that we are good, and we do not need to, for the Lord is the only true judge of goodness, and no one is good except whom he calls good.

Now we come to the last part of the text quoted in Isaiah: "Trees of righteousness, the planting of the Lord, that he might be glorified." The tree is organized, is it not, perfectly? Every tree is organized, and all on one general plan, although you cannot find any two alike. It is the infinite variety of God, but it is all perfection. Now we are to be called trees of righteousness, the planting of the Lord, that he might be glorified. In the natural tree we see the manifestation of the life of God, in its selection of proper nourishment. The roots take up that which is good for it, and reject that which is not good. It is a present thing. What gives life to everything on this earth? That is, what is the immediate cause? What is it that all vegetation depends upon?—The sun. Christ is the Sun of righteousness. We are to be trees of righteousness, therefore the sun that is shining upon us is the Sun of righteousness, and that is not far removed from the sunshine that we see, because that teaches us of it. More than that, it is the glory of God. It is the shining of God upon us. But now we speak simply of light which comes to us in this world. What is it that is the life of the tree?—Sunshine. If light does not shine upon the tree, it will not grow. There will be no life there. So Christ says, "I am the light of the world."

Light is life. "In him was life, and the life was the light of men." His life comes to us now, and life is power. You can see that in the sun; the power of the sun draws innumerable tons of water into the skies every day. Light is life and power in the tree. Why is it that the tree grows, and is just what it ought to be?—Because every ray of light that shines to it is received. This brings the sap, the nourishment, food, to every part of the tree, and causes it to grow. The tree simply takes every ray of light that comes to it. Suppose we were to do just the same way, then we would grow trees of righteousness.

The tree does not reject the sun nor a single ray of light, but all that comes to it, it takes gladly and absorbs, taking it into itself. That light is life, so that the tree is perfectly organized. Just so with us, if we will simply drink in the light, and that is the life of Christ. Then God will live in us, and will chose for us just the same as in the tree. We do not know anything, but he will think for us. What does he say?—Call upon him while he is near. How near is he?—"In thy mouth and in thy heart." "Let the wicked forsake his way, and the unrighteous man his thoughts: and let him return unto the Lord, and he will have mercy upon him; and to our God, for he will abundantly pardon. For my thoughts are not your thoughts, neither are your ways my ways, saith the Lord." If a man forsake his ways and his thoughts, what is there left of him?—Nothing.

What ways and what thoughts, then, are to be ours?—God's. Can I do as God does?—No. Can I set myself to thinking God's thoughts?—No. But he will think in us just what he wants us to think. He will not think for us such infinite thoughts as he thinks for himself, for he has not made us infinite; but he will think in us everything that he desires us to think, and will work in us perfectly to will and to do his good pleasure. Then we will be organized, reorganized, made new. It is God thinking and acting in us. We read yesterday: "Because that, when they knew God, they glorified him not as God, neither were thankful: but became vain in their reasonings, and their foolish heart was darkened." Rom.1:21. ("For the weapons of our warfare are not carnal, but mighty through God to the pulling down of strongholds); casting down *reasonings* and *every high thing that exalted itself against the knowledge of God*, and bringing into captivity every thought, to the obedience of Christ." The wisdom of this world is foolishness with God. Then when men think for themselves, not perfectly submitting to God, that he may think in them, just to that extent they are fools, no matter how learned. But when a man will yield soul and body to God, the Spirit of God will cast down these human reasonings, which are but vain imaginations, and the wisdom of God alone will be manifested. Now if God should think in every one of us assembled in General Conference, would there be any mistakes made? Would there be any haphazard work?—No. He would think the same thing in all of us. All are made in different phases. He has made no two trees of the forest alike, and he has made no two of us alike; but coming together with God thinking in each of us, there would not be any human wisdom, but only the wisdom of the Spirit of God. Then everything would be done exactly right, and nothing would be done that ought not to be done. The command to us is explicit: "If any man speak, let him speak as the oracles of God."—When? Is it only when he gets up and gives testimony in meeting? Is it not just as well when he engages in business?—Certainly; for there is no limit. Then of course we must speak differently from what we have been speaking, for we must confess that many things have heretofore been spoken at random. How often we hear the brethren say, when they are not sure about some action or suggestion, "We have acted according to the best light we have." Now what is "the best light we have"?—It is Christ, the light of the world, the wisdom of God; and he says, "Whosoever followeth me shall not walk in darkness, but shall have the light of life." Then whoever follows absolutely the best light he has, need never be in doubt.

Now one question: Since such certainty is possible for us, do we not assume a great and fearful responsibility when we venture to go ahead in what we call the Lord's work, without knowing to a certainty that it is God himself that is doing it. Dare we do so in this Conference? Shall we not rather allow the Lord to organize us, by filling us with his Spirit? Then Christ will be our wisdom and our strength, as well as our righteousness.

Study Number Ten
(Sunday Afternoon, February 28, 1897)

We have come to the closing verses of the second chapter of Hebrews; there is where we have read to:—

Forasmuch then as the children are partakers of flesh and blood, he also himself likewise took part of the same.

What for?—That he might destroy him that had the power of death. And do what?—Deliver. Deliver whom?—Those who were all their lifetime subject to bondage. And what was their bondage?—Fear; they were frightened, terrorized. Who is it that has the power of death?—Satan. How does he go about?—As a roaring lion. There is something fearful, something terrorizing, about a lion's roar. So he terrorizes and holds people in bondage by his roaring. What brings death?—Sin. How does sin bring death? Does it pick it up and carry it along as something apart from itself? "Lust, when it hath conceived, bringeth forth sin, and sin, when it is full grown, bringeth forth death." So sin carries death in itself, for sin is death. It is fear that brings men to bondage. Christ died that he might deliver from what?—From fear of death.

Wherefore, holy brethren, partakers of the heavenly calling, consider the Apostle and High Priest of our profession, Christ Jesus.

What is the particular thing we shall consider about him?—He is faithful. He suffered, being tempted, but he was faithful to him that appointed him. We are to consider him on that account. It is the same thought that is expressed in the twelfth chapter, where it says:—

For consider him that endured such contradiction of sinners against himself, lest ye be wearied and faint in your minds. Ye have not yet resisted unto blood.

Consider him, lest ye be weary and faint in your minds. Now, if we had to consider Christ simply as he was eighteen hundred years ago when he was tempted and did not yield, but was faithful,—if it were simply to look at his example, and try to imitate it, would we not become weary and faint?

How can you be like him?

(A voice) "By beholding we become changed."

Of what was he made partaker?

(A voice) Flesh and blood.

To what was he like?—His brethren in all things. And where is he still?

(A voice) In our flesh.

"The Word was made flesh, and dwelt among us." When did the Word cease to be made flesh?

(A voice) He was made so; and whatsoever God does shall be forever.

Very well. The Word was made flesh, and suffered. We have one perfect instance of it in the flesh, without any failure, simply to show what it is possible for God to do in flesh. Now we read that he suffered, being tempted. There is a verse that comes to my mind, 1 Pet. 4:1:—

"Forasmuch then as Christ hath suffered for us in the flesh, arm yourselves likewise with the same mind."

How can we arm ourselves with the same mind? The Word tells us: "Let this mind be in you, which was also in Christ Jesus." Just let it be so. There is one of the let-it-be's, one of God's creative words. Where do you find that word first?—First chapter of Genesis. "Let there be light." "Let the waters be gathered together." "Let the earth bring forth grass." "Let the waters bring forth abundantly." And what invariably followed?—"And it was so." So when we have the Word of the Lord, "Let this mind be in you," what will be the result if we receive it as God's Word?—It will be so. I say, Lord, amen, even so, let it be; and it is so. That is not simply a form of speech.

Forasmuch then as Christ hath suffered for us in the flesh, arm yourselves likewise with the same mind: for he that hath suffered in the flesh hath ceased from sin; that he no longer should live the rest of his time in the flesh to the lusts of men, but to the will of God.

We might feel like saying about this as the Jews once did to Christ's words: "This is an hard saying; who can hear it?" Who can hear it? "He that hath suffered in the flesh hath ceased from sin; that he no longer should live the rest of his time in the flesh to the lusts of men, but to the will of God." Of course that depends on a person's mind as to whether that is a desirable position or not. I can speak for myself that I know a good deal about the time as a matter of fact, when I did not regard that as desirable at all in ceasing from sin. Afterward I did not want to sin very much, but just a little. That seemed all right; I thought that was desirable; it was pleasing to me. I did not want to be a very bad sinner—in fact, I did not want to be called a sinner at all; but I did not want to cease from sin. Now, that is my public confession. I do not know whether any of you would duplicate it or not.

(Voices) I can.

Now here is a way by which if any one thinks more than that is desirable, that may be obtained; and if he does not think it is desirable, of course he will never obtain it. Christ hath suffered, being tempted, and is able to succor them that are tempted. Whoever arms himself with the same mind, by letting it be in him, and desires to be freed from sin so greatly that he is willing to endure suffering in the flesh in the struggle, may cease from sin. Christ suffered for us in the flesh being tempted. That is to say, his resistance of sin was so real, so powerful, the sin that was presented to him to resist was so strong, that it drew on the very fibers of his body, his very existence. How did he resist?—By faith. He struggled,—there was that which caused him suffering in the flesh because of the sin in the flesh.

Now let us read Isa.40:1,2: "Comfort ye, comfort ye my people, saith the Lord." Here is a message of comfort. We have referred to this chapter several times before, and we have found that its special application is now, because it contains the message that is to prepare the way of the Lord when he shall come with his reward. So to us apply the words, "Comfort ye, comfort ye my people, saith your God. Speak comfortably to Jerusalem," literally, "speak to the heart of Jerusalem," that is, so that they will understand, "and cry unto her, that her warfare is accomplished, that her iniquity is pardoned: for she hath received of the Lord's hand double for all her sins." What has she received double?—Mercy; because when the Lord pardons sins, gives grace to pardon, he does not measure it to fit the exact size and need. No, "where sin abounded, grace did much more abound." There is more than enough. "Return unto your God, and he will abundantly pardon;" as the margin has it, "multiply to pardon." "Cry unto her, that her warfare is accomplished." Here is something that is to be told to the people—Your warfare is accomplished. Does that mean that men may now sit down and have an easy time?—Oh, no; far from it; it means action. It means the taking of the victory that has been gained. Christ has accomplished the warfare; therefore what are you to do?—Rejoice in it. How can you rejoice in it?—By faith. Well, what is meant by that—by having victory in him? We get victory because his victory is our victory. His victory is our victory, because he gained it for us, and we get the benefit of it by allowing him to dwell in us in his fullness. The enemy is just as powerless against Christ in us, as he was against Christ eighteen hundred years ago.

Christ has gained the victory,—complete, perfect, absolute. He did no sin. He did not know sin in the sense of doing it; but he knew it in the power of it. Christ knows the power of sin better than anybody in this house, because he resisted to the utmost, and we have not. Now when one sets out to resist sin to the utmost, he will know the power of sin as he never knew it before, because if he lets himself be swept along, he will never know the power at all; but when he sets out to resist sin to the utmost extent, he will know the full power of it. Christ knows the power; he has gained the victory, complete, spoiled principalities and powers, and taken the weapons from the enemy. If we are in bondage, then, what are we in bondage to?—Sin. What is it that puts us in bondage?—Fear. There is no need of it, because liberty has been proclaimed, and when the

Lord proclaims liberty, there is liberty. The Lord stands and cries to the captives, "Liberty." Now when the Lord cries, Liberty, there is liberty. But to how many has he proclaimed liberty?—To all that are bound. Christ has brought liberty, absolute freedom. Men were in bondage to sin; Christ has brought absolute freedom from sin to every individual in the world; and he has taken the one who had the power of sin, the author of sin, the originator of sin, and spoiled him, made a show of him; so that he had no power at all in Christ's hand. With Christ how much power has Satan?—None at all. His power is gone. In any contest with Christ he has no power at all. He is helpless.

Here is a contest, here is a battle; two armies drawn up; here is one army well armed; that is, they have access to the best armor, their magazines are full, they are well equipped, and everything is perfect. The other army has nothing, and they are cowed, defeated. What would you think of this well-equipped army to let itself be taken captive by the other? It would be very foolish.

The message is that the warfare in every particular has been accomplished, has been fought, and won, absolutely. That is a thing for us to believe. Now if we believe that all the time, who is going to be foolish enough to be defeated? For do you suppose—is it possible that any man, believing and knowing that a foe with whom he had to contend was completely defeated, would be taken captive by him?—He could not.

Now arm yourself with the same mind. The devil has learned perfectly Christ's power. He has contested that, he knows it. He knows perfectly well that he cannot affect him in the slightest particular. Then when it is demonstrated to the devil's satisfaction that we are armed with Christ's mind, that we have encased ourselves in him, he will know that he can do nothing with us.

I do not mean to say that the devil will go away, and never come back again, because he has had so much experience with human kind that he knows that if he finds them on their guard one time, the next time he will very likely find them off. Because here is the way with us: when we have gained one victory, we get so elated over it that we begin to spend all our time thinking about it, and then we lose the next one. We think, "Now I am getting pretty good. I have learned how to do it; now I can gain victories all the time; I am all right." But are we good?—No; it is not I who gained the victory, but Christ. We have no right to take credit to ourselves. No man can ever in his Christian experience say that he is better than he once was; but he can acknowledge Christ's presence and power in him, and give to him the glory. Suppose I gain a victory, it is Christ who did it; it was not I. I could not do it; but the thing is done. Because the work is all of God, no man can boast. We are not to keep looking back to see how much progress we have made, but keep looking forward and upward to see how much greater things God has to show us.

Now, about arming ourselves with the same mind. "Let this mind be in you." That is, let Christ himself be in you; let Christ dwell in you. On these words, "Comfort ye," turn to the fourteenth chapter of John, sixteenth and eighteenth verses: "I will pray the Father, and he shall give you another Comforter." Now that word Comforter is from the very same Greek word that is used in 1John 2:1: "If any man sin, we have an advocate with the Father." That word "advocate" is identical with this word "Comforter." So that verse should read, "If any man sin, we have a Comforter with the Father, Jesus Christ the righteous." Now returning to the passage in John: "And he shall give you another Comforter, that he may abide with you forever; even the Spirit of truth; whom the world cannot receive, because it seeth him not, neither knoweth him; but ye know him; for he dwelleth with you, and shall be in you. I will not leave you comfortless: I will come to you." Christ says: I will not leave you orphans: I will come to you. Now, when does he mean that he will come?

Elder A. F. Ballenger: "When spoken, when did it mean?"

Well, we can answer that. It meant the same thing to those who heard it that it does to us. The same thing that was spoken to them is spoken to us, for the Word is a living Word. Now when will Christ come, when does he come, and how does he come to us according to this promise?—By the Spirit. Christ's promise to send the Holy Spirit was his proof of the statement that he would not leave us lone orphans, but would come to us. The Spirit, then, is Christ's representative on earth, and Christ comes and dwells in us by the Spirit. So he says, he shall take of mine, and show them to you. We are well provided with comfort. We have a Comforter with the Father, Jesus Christ the righteous; that assures an open communication at the end of the line; and we have also "another Comforter" with us, to abide with us forever, so that the communication is open all along the line. "For through him we both have access by one Spirit unto the Father." The Spirit dwelling in us brings Christ himself to dwell in us; and he in whom Christ dwells by the Spirit, is armed with the same mind that Christ was, is he not?

Question:—These two Comforters agree, do they not?

Of course they do. It is all the same comfort; for it is by the other Comforter that Christ dwells in us. Do you believe it?

(A voice) Yes, it is so.

How do you know it is so? The world cannot receive him, but you know him. How do you know him?—"He dwelleth in you, and shall be in you." When Christ is made in us righteousness, what is that righteousness?—Absence from sin; "what fellowship hath righteousness with unrighteousness?" Then Christ is made unto us freedom from sin; are we willing to accept him as that? But this is not all. He is made unto us wisdom. What fellowship has wisdom with ignorance? "In him are hid all the treasures of wisdom and knowledge." Jesus Christ is the wisdom of God and the power of God. Then how can a man, if he believes the Lord, and believes that this is all for us,—how can we (it is a practical thing for us here as delegates)—how can we go on in the dark as to what we ought to do, any more than we can go on living in sin? Christ may dwell in our hearts by faith, so that we may be filled with all the fullness of God. That is a good deal. Then why should we not allow God to manifest himself in us for all that he desires to do with us? Remember that we are not able to say anything as of ourselves, but "our sufficiency is of God." While a man holds himself to this, there is no danger at all. There is no danger in truth. There is no danger in accepting the truth. There never was a man in this world who was fanatical because he believed the Bible.

We have the promise of wisdom. Not only is Christ our righteousness, but our wisdom. What, then, is the use of our coming together and guessing about things? What is the use of a company of delegates coming together, and using their own human judgment, and then calling their conclusions the will of the Lord? Brethren, there is no need of a single mistake being made in this Conference. There is no need of a single thing being done from first to last that will ever have to be taken back. But I am afraid there will be; for there has never yet been a Conference among us where there was nothing done that had to be taken back. As I have been absent and have read the Conference reports in the BULLETIN, and seen that this one was to go here, and that one to go there, and then in the next number seen the recommendations reversed, and then when the Conference was over, and we received the *Review*, and would find that some of the recommendations were rescinded and others changed, I have wondered what was the use of wasting so much time in making the first decisions. There never has been a time in our history when mistakes have not been made; but that is no reason why we should go on at haphazard. "If any man speak, let him speak as the oracles of God." That would save much time in our councils. Whoever talks in this Conference, recommending any plan, ought first to be so well acquainted with God that he knows his will in that particular, and then the brethren will recognize it as such, and there will be no discussion over it. And thus, when we act, we may know that it is just the thing that God would have us do. Now when there is a possibility of knowing just exactly what the Lord would have done, what fearful responsibility rests upon the man that goes ahead and does not know. If we say that we don't know how to speak as the oracles of God, he tells us that he will pour out his Spirit upon us, and make known his words unto us. What, then, is the thing for us to do, brethren?

Study Number Eleven
(Monday Afternoon, February 22, 1897)

Hebrews 3:1-6: Wherefore, holy brethren, partakers of the heavenly calling, consider the Apostle and High Priest of our profession, Christ Jesus; who was faithful to him that appointed him, as also Moses was faithful in all his house. For this man was counted worthy of more glory than Moses, inasmuch as he who hath builded the house, hath more honor than the house. For every house is builded by some man; but he that built all things is God. And Moses verily was faithful in all his house, as a servant, for a testimony of those things which were to be spoken after; but Christ as a son over his own house; whose house are we, if we hold fast the confidence and the rejoicing of the hope firm unto the end.

We will spend a few moments in seeing what the text says. Who are we to consider?—Christ, the Apostle, and High Priest of our profession. What was the characteristic of him?—He was faithful. He was as faithful as whom?—As Moses. That was a good recommendation for Moses. To whom was he faithful?—To Him that appointed him. And who was he that appointed him?—God, the Father. And Moses was faithful—where?—In all his house. In whose house?—The house of God. In what capacity was he faithful?—As a servant. Christ was faithful in what capacity?—As a son. Over what?—Over his house. Christ is a son over whose house?—God's house. Not over his own house, but over God's house, the same house in which Moses was faithful. In the Revised Version the word "own" is very properly omitted.

Moses was faithful in all God's house as a servant, and Christ was faithful as a son. Christ was faithful as a son over God's house, and that house was composed of whom?—Of us, provided what?—Provided we hold fast the confidence, and the rejoicing of the hope, firm unto the end. Very good. Now, what is the prominent thing that we have here before us in these verses?—Faithfulness? Yes; the faithfulness of Christ, that is one thing; another thing is God's house. How many houses has God?

(Congregation) "One."

We can settle that, that God has but one house, without our own authority, by seeing what the house of God is. What is the house of God?—The church of God. Where do you find that?—In 1Tim.3:15, we find the statement that the house of God is the church of the living God. The house of God is the church of God. What other name have we besides the church, for God's house?—The body. We have that stated in the first chapter of Ephesians. The church is the body of Christ. How many bodies are there?—One body. This statement is found in the fourth chapter. That being the case, the matter is settled. The house is the church, the church is the body, and there is only one body. Then how many houses?—Only one house; one church. Therefore the house in which Moses was so faithful, is identical with the one in which Christ is faithful. The church in the wilderness is the same church that God has today.

In 1Pet.2:4,5 we read that, coming to Christ "as unto a living stone, disallowed indeed of men, but chosen of God, and precious, ye also as living stones are built up a spiritual house, an holy priesthood, to offer up spiritual sacrifices acceptable to God by Jesus Christ." Coming to whom?—To Christ. What is he?—The living stone. You read of that stone in the twenty-eighth of Isaiah: "Behold, I lay in Sion for a foundation, a stone, a tried stone, a precious corner stone, a sure foundation." Not only is he the corner stone, but the whole foundation. "For other foundation can no man lay, than that is laid." And what is that?—Jesus Christ. So the foundation is Christ. Now, coming unto him as unto the living stone, what is wrought for us?—"Ye also as living stones." What is the nature of the foundation?—It is a live stone. When any one comes and settles down upon that stone, what effect does it have upon him?—It makes him living. Every stone that is put upon that stone becomes living. It partakes of the nature of the foundation. The Life of the foundation comes up into it. "Ye also as living stones, are built up a spiritual house."

Now turn to the second chapter of Ephesians, and you find the nature of this house. It is a stone house, but such a stone house as you nor I nor any one else ever saw any man build. In Ephesians we have another part of this story:—

> [Christ] came and preached peace to you which were afar off, and to them that were nigh. For through him we both have access by one Spirit unto the Father. Now therefore ye are no more strangers and foreigners, but fellow citizens with the saints, and of the household of God; and are built upon the foundation of the apostles and prophets, Jesus Christ himself being the chief corner stone.

A household consisting of sons and daughters is often spoken of in the Bible as a house. We speak of the house of David. "And are built upon the foundation of the apostles and prophets;" that is the foundation laid by them, "Jesus Christ himself being the chief corner stone." Now notice that as the stones become alive as soon as they are placed upon the living Stone, so the house is alive and grows. In Christ "all the building fitly framed together groweth unto an holy temple in the Lord: in whom ye also are builded together for an habitation of God through the Spirit." That is the same thought that we had yesterday—Christ dwelling in our hearts by faith; the reception of the Spirit of God brings Christ into the heart. In promising the Spirit, he says, I will not leave you comfortless; I will come to you. And so he says in the fourteenth chapter of John, that not only I, but my Father also will come and dwell with that man, and abide with him. So here we have the statement that we are builded together for an habitation of God through the Spirit. What is the habitation of God—what is the place where God dwells?—The temple. The house, or, in other words, the church, the body as a whole, is the temple of God. But in order that it may be so as a whole, what is necessary? What do we have in the third and sixth chapters of First Corinthians?—"Know ye not that ye are the temple of the Holy Ghost?" or, "that ye are the temple of the living God?" So that when these different living stones—the different individuals—becomes thus filled full, then the whole mass of living stones is filled, and the whole thing becomes the temple of God. When does this take place, that is, at what time? Is it in the future that the church is to become the temple of the living God, an habitation of God through the Spirit?

(Voices) It is now.

Are you sure of that? You must not be hasty in that statement. Let us examine. It says, "ye are." "Ye *are* builded." Shall we take it that after the house is built, the Lord will come and look it over, and if it suits him he will move in?—No; he is the foundation; he is there first, and the house is built on him, and in him, and through him, and he is in the house. That is a fact.

Now, if we are all agreed that the house of God, his temple, his church, is for his present habitation, let us see what are the characteristics of God's house, his temple. In the temple of God, as the prominent feature of it, is the throne of God. God's throne is in his temple, and the temple itself is a living temple. Here we have the temple of God, a living house, composed of living stones, in which God himself dwells by his Spirit; and you have said that that must be the case now.

Let us turn to the first chapter of Ezekiel, and notice the statements that are there made concerning the throne of God:—

> Now it came to pass in the thirtieth year, in the fourth month, in the fifth day of the month, as I was among the captives by the river of Chebar, that the heavens were opened, and I saw visions of God. In the fifth day of the month, which was the fifth year of king Jehoiachin's captivity, the word of the Lord came expressly unto Ezekiel the priest, the son of Buzi, in the land of the Chaldeans by the river Chebar; and the hand of the Lord was there upon him.
>
> And I looked, and, behold, a whirlwind came out of the north, a great cloud, and a fire enfolding itself, and a brightness was about it, and out of the midst thereof as the color of amber, out of the midst of fire. Also out of the midst thereof came the likeness of four living creatures. And this was their appearance; they had the likeness of a man. And every one had four faces, and every one had four wings. And their feet were straight feet; and the sole of their feet was like the sole of a calf's foot; and they sparkled like the color of burnished brass. And they had the hands of a man under their wings on their four sides; and they four had their faces and their wings. Their wings were joined one to another; they turned not when they

went; they went every one straight forward. As for the likeness of their faces, they four had the face of a man, and the face of a lion, on the right side: and they four had the face of an ox on the left side; they four also had the face of an eagle. Thus were their faces: and their wings were stretched upward; two wings of every one were joined one to another, and two covered their bodies. And they went every one straight forward: whither the spirit was to go, they went; and they turned not when they went. As for the likeness of the living creatures, their appearance was like burning coals of fire, and like the appearance of lamps: it went up and down among the living creatures; and the fire was bright and out of the fire went forth lightning. And the living creatures ran and returned as the appearance of a flash of lightning.

Now I behold the living creatures, behold one wheel upon the earth by the living creatures, with his four faces. The appearance of the wheels and their work was like unto the color of a beryl: and they four had one likeness: and their appearance and their work was as it were a wheel in the middle of a wheel. When they went, they went upon their four sides: and they turned not when they went. As for their rings, they were so high that they were dreadful; and their rings were full of eyes round about them four. And when the living creatures went, the wheels went by them: and when the living creatures were lifted up from the earth, the wheels were lifted up. Whithersoever the spirit was to go, they went, thither was their spirit to go; and the wheels were lifted up over against them: for the spirit of the living creature was in the wheels. When those went, those went; and when those stood, these stood; and when those were lifted up from the earth, the wheels were lifted up over against them: for the spirit of the living creature was in the wheels. And the likeness of the firmament upon the heads of the living creature was as the color of the terrible crystal, stretched forth over their heads above. And under the firmament were their wings straight, the one toward the other: every one had two, which covered on this side, and every one had two, which covered on that side, their bodies. And when they went, I heard the noise of their wings, like the noise of great waters, as the voice of the Almighty, the voice of speech, as the noise of an host: when they stood, they let down their wings. And there was a voice from the firmament that was over their heads, when they stood, and had let down their wings.

And above the firmament that was over their heads was the likeness of a throne, as the appearance of a sapphire stone: and upon the likeness of the throne was the likeness as the appearance of a man above upon it. And I saw as the color of amber, as the appearance of fire round about within it, from the appearance of his loins even upward, and from the appearance of his loins even downward, I saw as it were the appearance of fire, and it had brightness round about. As the appearance of the bow that is in the cloud in the day of rain, so was the appearance of the brightness round about. This was the appearance of the likeness of the glory of the Lord.

Here, then, we have the best description that human language could frame, of the throne of God. Now, if every one of us, or the whole body, the church, is the temple of God, then of course the throne of God is in his temple. And what kind of a temple is it?—A living house. What is the characteristic of his throne?—It is a living throne, composed of living creatures. It is all alive. From the throne of God comes life, the river of life. That is the source of life, infinite life. The throne of God is life because just the same as when we come to the living foundation we are made alive, so everything that is in God's presence must be living. His presence gives life, and his throne is a living throne, for his house is a living house.

Take the twentieth verse: "Whithersoever the Spirit was to go, they went." Who went?—The living creatures that form the throne. Whithersoever his Spirit is to go, they go. How long did it take for the order to reach them, and for them to go to this place or that? Does it say anything about any order being given?—No. Then what was it—whithersoever the Spirit was to go, their spirit was to go? How could that be? What does that show us?—That the spirit that was in them was the Spirit of God. There is but one Spirit in the whole. Whithersoever the Spirit was to go, their spirit was to go because the Spirit of life was in them; so that God's throne is, we may say, alive with his presence, just tingling, active with the presence of his Spirit pervading it all. God thinks, he wishes to go; and instantly he is there; for we must not think of God as shut up to one fixed place—the throne went and came back like a flash of lightning. They went hither and thither; but they turned not when they went; whithersoever the Spirit was to go they went. That is the perfection of motion. That is the perfection of organization.

Now what do we have on earth as the most perfect human organization?—A well-drilled army is the most perfect organization on earth. You take the German army, for instance. A man in one place can give the word, can press an electric button, and the whole mass of troops will instantly be in motion. They may be around the barracks, but they will instantly fall into their places, every man in his place, and they will march at the word of command. There you will see them marching like one man, and suddenly they stop; or, they wheel and go in another direction, just as though there was but one man. What causes these different movements?—The word of command. How does it come about that all these men move together as one man?—By organization. Yes; but the drill comes in this: those men there in the ranks have been trained to hold their minds ready to listen to the word of command, so that, when the officer thinks a certain evolution, and puts his thought into a word, and as soon as the word goes out, what does it produce?—It produces that same thought in the mind of each man in the ranks. For some thought must precede the action, so that they think his thought, only it takes an appreciable length of time for his thought to become theirs. But their minds are subordinated to his mind.

Now, suppose those soldiers were simply dreaming of their own affairs, some of one thing and some of another, would they have that perfect drill?—No, sir. When a body of men are drilling, their bodies are set; there is a sort of stolidity there, so far as that is concerned. They are simply there as machines, with no business to have any mind at all; the less mind of their own that they have, the better machines they are; and that is all they want to be, so that the mind of the commanding officer will be put into them, and they move. He thinks for them. Just as he thinks, they do. That is the perfection of military drill; that is the most perfect organization that is known.

(Voice) No, sir. The church of Christ is the most perfect organization on earth? Is it not?

The church of Christ is not a human organization. The army is the most perfectly organized thing that the human mind can conceive or bring to perfection. When the word is given, then the next one gives the command to the different parts of that division, and they move all together, perfectly and harmoniously. But it is only a machine, consequently there is no individuality; there is only one mind in the whole army. That is accomplished by hard work,—a hard, arbitrary thing; and after years of that, the fact is seen that the man is useless for anything else—for any other kind of work. He must take orders from somebody else; he is simply a machine. That is the result of one human mind being subject to another human mind.

But here, on the other hand, we have God's organization, his house, the perfect body. Do we find in it one man's mind controlling another man's mind, as in the army?—No. There we have mind acting upon mind; here in this we have, it is true, only one mind, but it is the mind of God, the Spirit of God. "Whither the Spirit was to go, they went; and they turned not when they went," because the Spirit of life, the Spirit of God was in them. That is the perfect organization. You said that this thing of God dwelling in his temple, in this living house, is a thing not for the future, but for the present time. Do you hold to that still?—Yes. Another question: Do you see any such perfection of organization anywhere on earth where men without drill as in the army, move as one man?—No. What is the conclusion, then?

Let us consider the matter closely. Here are two statements which you yourselves have made: You have said, having read the scriptures as to what the temple of God is, what it is for,—the habitation of God through the Spirit,—that the time is now, has been a long time, of course, when God would dwell in his people in this living house. We have read here what is the characteristic of that temple of God, when God dwells in it, as shown by the movement of his throne,—perfect, spontaneous action, because the Spirit of God was their spirit. They had the same Spirit, his spirit was through them, so that when the Spirit thought, they thought the same thing. Then you have stated, as a second thing, that you never saw on earth any such unity, any such perfection of movement, in any body of people.

Study Number Eleven • 83

(A voice) Were not the apostles thus united at the time of Pentecost?

O, yes; but we have not seen them. What now is the conclusion?—Simply this: That God is not dwelling in this temple in his fullness, or else we are not letting it be built into a temple just as he wants it. I was reading a statement here just after class yesterday, which I will read to you:—

To the prophet, the wheel within the wheel, the appearances of living creatures connected with them, all seem intricate and unexplainable. But the hand of infinite wisdom is seen among the wheels, and perfect order is the result of its work. Every wheel works in perfect harmony with every other. I have been shown that human instrumentalities seek after too much power, and try to control the work themselves. They leave the Lord God, the mighty Worker, too much out of their methods and plans, and do not trust everything to him in regard to the advancement of the work.

When is it that we leave God too much out of our plans—under what circumstances?—When we do not trust everything to him.

No one should fancy that he is able to manage these things which belong to the great I AM. God in his providence is preparing a way so that the work may be done by human agents. Then let every man stand at his post of duty, to act his part for this time, and know that God is his Instructor.

Again:—

Christ breathed upon his disciples, and said, "Receive ye the Holy Ghost." Christ is represented by his Holy Spirit today in every part of his great moral vineyard. He will give the inspiration of his Holy Spirit to all those who are of a contrite spirit. Let there be more dependency upon the efficiency of the Holy Spirit, and far less upon human agencies. I am sorry to say that at least some have not given evidence that they have learned the lesson of meekness and lowliness in the school of Christ. They do not abide in Christ, they have no vital connection with him. They are not directed by the wisdom of Christ, through the impartation of his Holy Spirit. Then I ask you, How can we regard these men as faultless in judgment? They may be in responsible positions, but they are living separate from Christ. They have not the mind of Christ, and do not learn daily of him. Yet in some cases their judgment is trusted, and their counsel is regarded as the wisdom of God.

That means every one who is not thus moved by the divine power.

When human agents choose the will of God, and are conformed to the character of Christ, Jesus acts through their organs and faculties.

There we have exactly the thing we have read here in the Bible. God acts through the organs and faculties of the members of his church, when all are subject to him. Have we had that as yet demonstrated among us? I do not know the heart of any man. I do not say that there have not been many who have let the Lord use their organs and faculties completely; but have we, in this our work, seen Christ in our little experience, acting through the organs and faculties of the mind and body of his people in this way?

They put aside all selfish pride, all manifestations of superiority, all arbitrary exactions, and manifest the meekness and lowliness of Christ. It is no more themselves that live and act, but it is Christ that lives and acts through them.

In closing, I would like to ask, What practical use are we going to make of this lesson? What must we seek in order to be God's perfect temple?

Study Number Twelve
(Tuesday Afternoon, February 23, 1897)

"Behold I and the children which God hath given me." That is one of the quotations in the second chapter of Hebrews. Let us finish the statement: "Behold I and the children whom the Lord hath given me are for signs and for wonders in Israel from the Lord of hosts, which dwelleth in Mount Zion." Isa.8:18.

Yesterday we considered briefly the house of God, the temple of the living God, God's church, God's building—ourselves—"for an habitation of God through the Spirit." There is a good deal of talk in the religious world about the Real Presence. There is such a real presence, the presence of God, and that real presence is to be in every child of God, and in the church. That real presence is through the Spirit. We saw by studying the vision which Ezekiel had of God and his throne, the nature of whatever place where God dwells in: wherever God is, there is life. Even when God came down upon Mount Sinai it could not stand still. The whole mountain was moving. It could not keep still while God was upon it, for there was life there. The whole throne is a living throne, composed of living creatures, and they come and go like a flash of lightning.

Now note, every one of these living creatures was different from every other one—different faces, different appearance, different shape, and they were sent with their faces different ways; but in spite of that there was not a shadow, a suggestion, or a thought of any lack of unity in their movement. Just as one body they moved this way or that way. They turned not when they went. And why?—For "whithersoever the spirit was to go, they went." But how could that be?—"The spirit of life," as it reads in the margin, "was in them." So, necessarily, "whithersoever the spirit was to go, they went," because the Spirit was in them. We contrasted that with the highest manifestation of human organization possible on earth—an army—that all move as one man. But there must be a word of command. But how is it that these men, that those evolutions, those movements, can be made, accomplished with these men?

(A voice) They have the mind of the commander.

Yes, but how did they get that?—They are drilled. Did they drill separately?—O, no; first they had to be all brought to one place, under one man. They get orders from him, get accustomed to the word of command, and then by continual exercise get so that they move almost involuntarily at the word of command.

Now then, God has an army on this earth, because we read here of the "Captain of our salvation." God is "the Lord of hosts."

He has a body on this earth, but he does not gather all his children together in one place to drill them, and he is not obliged to. That is an advantage of God's organization over human organizations; for, further, every man in that human organization must look to one man and recognize his authority, and submit his mind to that other man's mind. But every man's mind is to be submitted to God alone. God is supreme; God has the sole right to control every man's mind, because the mind of God is the only true, correct, and wise mind.

Talk about the harmony of reason and faith! They are just as wide apart as it is possible for two things to be. Faith is the utmost nonsense to human reason; it is foolishness, utter foolishness; and human reason is the baldest kind of nonsense to faith. They never can come together in this world. The weapons of our warfare are such as cast down human reason, "casting down reasonings." In the text it is called imaginations. It is all right either way, only the word is properly "reason." But human reason is only a figment, because there is nothing to it, so that when the human mind reasons, undirected by the Spirit of God, it is only imagination.

The Spirit of God, when allowed to work, casts down imaginations and every thing that exalts itself against the knowledge of God, and brings into captivity every thought to the obedience of Christ. Reason rests with God alone, and when a man puts himself fully into the hands of God, to be controlled, body, soul, and spirit, utterly controlled,—saying, I am only dust, and have nothing to do with myself; I belong to the Lord; now let him be my thought in my brain, and be my movement, my action; then that man's action will be right, and his thoughts will be right. "Commit thy ways unto the Lord, and thy thoughts shall be established."

Now, I say the Lord has a body on this earth. He has left here, as he has gone away, some of his children. He has left us here to represent him here on this earth, as individuals, as a church.

We are ambassadors for Christ, as though God did beseech you by us; we pray you in Christ's stead, be ye reconciled to God.

Now we may say we do that, but we do not do it at all, unless the same condition obtains in us that obtained in Christ. As preachers we may get up before congregations and say, We are ambassadors for Christ; and "we pray you in Christ's stead, be ye reconciled to God;" but we are not doing that unless we are occupying the same position that Christ occupied. What was that?—He allowed God to dwell in him. How fully?—"It pleased the Father that in him should all fullness dwell." Now the Spirit's desire for us is,—

That he would grant you, according to the riches of his glory, to be strengthened with might by his Spirit in the inner man; that Christ may dwell in your hearts by faith; that ye, being rooted and grounded in love, may be able to comprehend with all saints what is the breadth, and length, and depth, and height; and to know the love of Christ, which passeth knowledge, that ye might be filled with all the fullness of God. Eph.3:16–19.

When we stand in that place, we are indeed ambassadors for Christ, and God beseeches men by us.

The people on this earth say a great deal about organization. We cannot show them anything in that line. We do not begin to have so complete and perfect a system of organization as the Salvation Army has, or the Jesuit body of the Roman Catholic Church. We cannot teach the world anything about that. In the armies of the earth there is organization and uniformity of action as perfect as can be. The people know all about that, and they know how it is done too. But when God's people, here and there, and all over the world, a people professing in an especial way to be the people of God, having a special message to give to the people,—when they as individuals are filled with the Spirit of God, so that that picture of the throne of God is duplicated here on earth, God enthroned in the hearts of his people, so that whithersoever the Spirit is to go they go, do you not think that the world will see something wonderful in it? Will not God's children be for a sign, and a wonder to the people?

How is that brought about? What rules and regulations have you by which that is accomplished?—None. There will be the wonder. Let us read a few verses in the fifty-second chapter of Isaiah:—

Awake, awake; put on thy strength, O Zion; put on thy beautiful garments, O Jerusalem, the holy city; for henceforth there shall no more come into thee the uncircumcised and the unclean.... Now therefore, what have I here, saith the Lord, that my people is taken away for nought? they that rule over them make them to howl, saith the Lord; and my name continually every day is blasphemed. Therefore my people shall know my name [that is what we have been studying here] therefore they shall know in that day that I am he that doth speak: behold, it is I. How beautiful upon the mountains are the feet of him that bringeth good tidings, that publisheth peace; that bringeth good tidings of good, that publisheth salvation; that saith unto Zion, Thy God reigneth! Thy watchmen shall lift up the voice; with the voice together shall they sing: for they shall see eye to eye, when the Lord shall bring again Zion.

Break forth into joy, sing together, ye waste places of Jerusalem: for the Lord hath comforted his people, he hath redeemed Jerusalem. The Lord hath made bare his holy arm in the eyes of all the nations; and all the ends of the earth shall see the salvation of our God. [That means all of us.]

Depart ye, depart ye, go ye out from thence, touch no unclean thing; go ye out of the midst of her; be ye clean, that bear the vessels of the Lord.

How do we get this cleansing? O, we know that. We confess our sins, and "the blood of Jesus Christ cleanseth us from all sin." "Now are you clean through the word that I have spoken unto you," but not if we let the word lie, neglecting it.

For ye shall not go out with haste, nor go by flight: for the Lord will go before you; and the God of Israel will be your reward. Behold, my servant shall deal prudently.

That has been to me a blessed assurance of late,—"Behold, my servant shall deal prudently." Who is the servant of the Lord? O, you say, this is Christ. True, but "as he is, so are we in this world." Are we not servants of the Lord, too? Are we one with the Lord Jesus Christ? Then is not this promise to us? because whatever is to Christ, is to us, for we are heirs of God, and joint heirs with him. There is no promise to Christ, then, that he does not pass along and share with us. "Behold, my servant shall deal prudently." That will be characteristic of the servant of God. He will deal prudently. I am glad for that, because I know that I am one of the most imprudent persons in the world; and when I read that God, through faith, brings strength out of weakness, then I rejoice for this promise that "my servant shall deal prudently," and I am glad that God can work prudence even in me.

He shall be exalted and extolled, and be very high. As many were astonished at thee; his visage was so marred more than any man, and his form more than the sons of men: so shall he astonish many nations; the kings shall shut their mouths at him: for that which had not been told them shall they see; and that which they had not heard shall they consider. Who hath believed our report? and to whom is the arm of the Lord revealed? For he shall grow up before him as a tender plant, and as a root out of a dry ground; he hath no form nor comeliness; and when we shall see him, there is no beauty that we should desire him.

Here is the arm of the Lord revealed in the sight of the nations as power, so that all the ends of the earth see the salvation of God; so that nations shall be astonished, and kings will simply shut their mouths in wonder and amazement. What has not been told them, what they could not dream of even, they will see. They will see a power, without seeing the source of power. They will see a mighty power, and yet no great appearance or show of power. They will see perfect unity of action, and yet no man possessing or claiming authority.

Now, let me call your attention to the fortieth chapter of Isaiah. See another thing that is going to be done. We might study a long while before we could exhaust that fortieth chapter of Isaiah. It tells about—

The voice of him that crieth in the wilderness, Prepare ye the way of the Lord, make straight in the desert a highway for our God. Every valley shall be exalted, and every mountain and hill shall be made low; and the crooked shall be made straight, and the rough places plain.

That is, there is to be no crookedness in this work. It is to be perfectly straight and level. There is no going around in any crooked way, but it is to be done straight and plain before us. God's work is a straight work. It is not to get around something, nor to follow up men in all their devious ways of error. Not to follow men wherever they may go in their crookedness, and try to expose them, but to go straight ahead. The work of the Lord is a straight work. We are to mind our own business, and let other people do the dodging around. This tells us of the same thing that the fifty-second chapter did:—

The glory of the Lord shall be revealed, and all flesh shall see it together, for the mouth of Jehovah hath spoken it.

Now the lesson: Whose voice was heard in the wilderness?—John the Baptist's. But he did not complete this message, because it is to continue until the work is done—until the Lord comes. "Prepare ye the way of the Lord." He is coming. How is he coming?—He is coming with a strong hand, and his arm shall rule for him. Behold his reward is with him, and his work before him. He has not come yet. The work is going on still; that voice crying in the wilderness is still sounding, although not yet very loudly.

It is clear enough without any further spending of time, that our work is identical with that of John the Baptist. "Prepare ye the way of the Lord." Let us then read one verse in the third chapter of Matthew:—

In those days came John the Baptist, preaching in the wilderness of Judea, and saying, Repent ye: for the kingdom of heaven is at hand. For this is he that was spoken of by the prophet Esaias, saying, The voice of one crying in the wilderness, Prepare ye the way of the Lord, make his paths straight. And the same John had his raiment of camel's hair, and a leathern girdle about his loins; and his meat was locusts and wild honey. Then went out to him Jerusalem, and all Judea, and all the region round about Jordan.

Now, in the first place, as to John the Baptist himself, what kind of man was he? What characterized him?—He was filled with the Holy Ghost. What, therefore, must characterize those who proclaim this message, "Prepare ye the way of the Lord, and make straight in the desert a highway for our God."—They must be filled with the Spirit of God. Which is the greater, the beginning of a thing, or the end of a thing?—The end. Then just as surely as the Bible is true, when those who profess to give this message begin to give it, when, with the fullness of the Spirit and of the power of God, they proclaim this message of truth, people will flock to hear it by the thousands; in other words, the whole world's attention will be called to it, and they cannot help themselves. They will be compelled to hear it. They will not all accept it, we know that. But there will be a power which will attract the attention of the whole world, and the one thing that will be talked about from the lowest south to the highest north, and around the world everywhere, will be the truth of the Lord's coming, and the preparation to meet him. That will be the one thing that will absorb the attention of the world. They will be obliged to talk of that, because that will be the thing that will come to them with greater force than any other thing in the world that they hear. I do not say that it will continue very long, because when it goes with that power, then men will decide very soon, either one way or the other; they will yield to it, or else throw it away and give themselves no more concern about it. That is going to be done; that must be done. It will be done. I read another text. Isaiah fifty-five:—

Ho, every one that thirsteth, come ye to the waters and he that hath no money; come ye, buy, and eat; yea, come, buy wine and milk without money and without price.

Here is something that speaks to us.

Wherefore do ye spend money for that which is not bread? and your labor for that which satisfieth not? hearken diligently unto me, and eat ye that which is good, and let your soul delight itself in fatness. ...Behold I have given him [the one in whom the covenant was made] for a witness to the people.

Who is given for a witness unto the people?—Christ. Who is the commander? Who is the one who has authority?—Christ has authority and power. I have given him for a witness; for a leader. Is he accepted as being leader, and is he commander?

(A voice) Yes.

That remains to be seen. What does a commander do?—He gives orders. And to whom does he give orders?—To those who are to receive the orders. He gives the orders so that they can be understood, and if he is indeed the leader and commander of the people, then what about his commands?—They are obeyed; and that determines whether he is leader and commander, or not.

Behold, thou shalt call a nation that thou knowest not, and nations that knew not thee shall run unto thee because of the Lord thy God, and for the Holy One of Israel, for he hath glorified thee.

Now mark, they do not run unto us because of us, not because of our good, our glory, because we have none; but nations that know not us will run unto us because of the Holy One of Israel in the midst of his people, and because his presence in the midst has glorified the whole. We have it in the sixtieth chapter of Isaiah:—

Arise, shine, for thy light is come, and the glory of the Lord is risen upon thee. For, behold, the darkness shall cover the earth, and gross darkness the people: but the Lord shall rise upon thee, and his glory shall be seen upon thee. And the Gentiles shall come to thy light, and kings to the brightness of thy rising.

The same story is told all the way through. There is the work of the people of God. That is the way the truth is to go. It does not say that all these kings and nations and Gentiles that run will accept it, but an ensign is to be lifted up, as a standard, something that will *per force* attract the attention of every man, from the greatest king to the lowest peasant; they will look at it, and when they see it they can do as they please. That will be the proclamation of the truth to the world. Now we go to the world.

A. F. Ballenger.—"And get up a debate to get a crowd."

Yes; and we preach certain points of doctrine. We sharpen them to a very fine point, so that we can stick them into people, and prod them. Then we say that they have had the truth; they have had the light. Have they had the truth?—No. They have not had the truth unless they have seen the power and glory of the Lord Jesus Christ through the Spirit. When the truth has come to them in that way, then indeed they have had the truth, and they are responsible to God as to whether they accept it or reject it; and it will not be long until that is done.

I wonder if you believe these things. What are we here for, anyhow? to listen for an hour or three-quarters of an hour, and then go away and say, perchance, That was very clear today; that seemed to be quite plain; that was a very good lesson? Brethren, how long before we are going to wake up? How long are we going to play at believing the Lord.

Now I read yesterday, very hastily, because the time was about expired, one or two sentences, and I will read one or two of them again:—

Christ breathed upon the disciples and said, Receive ye the Holy Ghost. Christ is represented by his Holy Spirit today, in every part of his great moral vineyard.

But is he represented by his Holy Spirit in every one who professes to be laboring for him, in every part of the great moral vineyard? That is the question. It is for me as well as for you.

He will give the inspiration of his Holy Spirit to all who are of a contrite spirit. Let there be more dependence upon the efficiency of the Holy Spirit, and far less upon human agencies.—Special Test, No. 3, p.48.

It is speaking about men who do not abide in Christ, are not directed by the wisdom of Christ and the impartation of the Holy Spirit, and cannot be trusted as faultless in judgment. There is no man on earth whose judgment can be trusted. Christ alone is the leader; he can be trusted. Let him through the Spirit dwell in us, think in us, act in us, and then there will be a difference.

Yet in some cases their judgment is trusted, and their counsel is regarded as the wisdom of God. When human agents choose the will of God, and are conformed to the character of Christ, Jesus acts through their organs and faculties. It is no more themselves that live and act, but it is Christ that lives and acts in them.

Now I ask you if in that condition there will be any mistakes, and wrong moves made? Here on another page I read thus:—

The Lord is soon to work in greater power among us; but there is danger of allowing our impulses to carry us where the Lord would not want us to go.

We must not go a long distance without knowing where we are. Does it say that?—No. It says, "We must not make one step that we will have to retrace." Then we must do nothing of which we are in doubt; we must not do one thing that there is a possibility of our having to retrace. That is plain and reasonable. Very good. Now suppose here is a subject right here in Conference that we do not know whether it is right, or whether it is wrong. This is a practical question for us. Here is a matter of business, a resolution, or a nomination, or whatever may come up for consideration. We say we will do the best we can, but we are not absolutely sure as to whether it is right or wrong. Then we do not know but that we shall have to retract the action sometime. Then hadn't we better know, or wait until we find out? Let me read another statement:—

ONLY GOD'S PLANS TO BE FOLLOWED

You are not to limit the Holy one of Israel, whose power is of old, and whose ways are past finding out. If you mark out ways whereby you expect God to work, you will be disappointed. The kingdom of heaven cometh not with observation.

Yes; it comes in just the opposite way to what we expect it. How is the arm of the Lord to be revealed?—"For he shall grow up before him as a tender plant, and as a root out of a dry ground." You do not expect a tree to grow to any proportions out of the dry ground, in the sand. But that is the way the Lord does. The Lord says that his power is such that he takes the base things of the world, and things despised, yes, and the things that are not, and brings to naught the things that are. That is the power of God. He works just exactly contrary to the manner in which man expects him to work, Just contrary to human plans and human organization; because, as we said, Human reason and faith are direct opposites.

You are to leave God to work in his own way, and you must walk, not by sight, but by faith. God has a work to be done, and it is a very solemn, sacred work. It is not wise to follow plans of your own devising.

Then are we going to walk as wise men, or as fools? Here is something for every delegate here to consider, for all of us to get. We all agree that we have before us here in these scriptures what s to be the work of God.

How many times does the testimony say the Lord is soon to work with greater power? How many times have we said that there is coming a time when the power of the Pentecost will be seen? Is this going to come?—O, yes; but the way we do would remind one of what an old Baptist said in the days of Carey, when he was talking about going to the heathen. Said he, "Young man, when the Lord wants the heathen to be converted, he will convert them without any help from you or power,—that we will wake up some morning, and find him working with great power? I do not know of any way for us to expect the Lord to work with greater power for us

Study Number Twelve • 93

as a people than for us—as many as want to be in the work then—to let ourselves be in his hand as dust. We do not know anything at all. We are utterly helpless. Now let the Lord come in, and build us up anew,—organize us on his own new diving plan, on the model of the divine temple, and live and act and think through us in his own way. And when that is done, there will be mighty power. Now, if that is true, and that can be done, then are we obliged to wait ten years? or shall we plan beforehand, and let all the people know that at the next General Conference are we going to have the power of the Lord? Isn't it time now for the Lord to work?

I will read, if I can readily find it, a statement here:—

Unless those who can help in—[that means everywhere,] are aroused to a sense of their duty, they will not recognize the work of God when the loud cry of the third angel shall be heard. When light goes forth to lighten the earth, instead of coming up to the help of the Lord, they will want to bind about his work to meet their narrow ideas.

Now, brethren, the Lord does not ask us to go back to the past, or to doubt that he has been with us. he is with us. Thank the Lord, he has been with us all these years; but that does not mean that he has approved everything we have done. God has been with even the heathen. Shall the heathen therefore say, "I am all right?" If God had not been with me, I would not believing. But what has the Lord been with us all these years for?—O, he has been calling for us, and pleading that we would let him work in us. He has been with us; I thank him for that. He has been with us, and because he is with us still, brethren, let us give him full control of our minds and bodies, to work in us in any place where he may call us to work.

Let me tell you that the Lord will work in this last work very much one of the common order of things, and in a way that will be contrary to any human planning. There will be those among us who will always want to control the work of God, to dictate even what movements shall be made when the work goes forward under the direction of the angel who joins the third angel in the message to be given to the world.

I do not want to be one of them, do you? How are you going to know when the angel joins with the third angel, and the message foes with a loud cry? If we keep on as we have been going, we will not know. Is it not time, then, for us to stop, to call a halt, until we do know where we are, and let the Lord begin to use us now? It is our right and privilege, and I thank the Lord it need not take long.

How much more do we know, how much more does any man here think he knows, than the twelve apostles did after they had been personally with the Lord for three and one-half years? If any man thinks he knows as much, let him raise his hand. Either you do not think so, or you are modest. How many think we are better able to devise plans and carry them out than those twelve men were? Yet the Lord told them, "Tarry ye in the city of Jerusalem, until ye be endued with power from on high."

Now if they did not know enough to go about the work after they had been with Christ, and had done a work that we have never done,—worked with power, cast out devils, raised the dead, performed many miracles, and done more powerful preaching than any of us have ever done,—I say, if it was necessary for them to wait until the Spirit of God filled them that they might have wisdom to go forth to the work, what are we claiming if we presume to go forth to the work without doing the very same thing? It was not very long that they had to wait, only ten days.

And when the day of Pentecost was fully come, they were all with one accord in one place. And suddenly there came a sound from heaven as of a rushing mighty wind, and it filled all the house where they were sitting. And there appeared unto them cloven tongues like as of fire, and it sat upon each of them. And they were all filled with the Holy Ghost, and began to speak with other tongues, as the Spirit gave them utterance. And there were dwelling at Jerusalem Jews, devout men, out of every nation under heaven. Now when this was noised abroad, the multitude came together. Acts 2: 1–6.

When they got the Spirit, they had no difficulty in finding a congregation. "Behold, I and the children whom thou hast given me are for signs and wonders from the Lord of hosts, which dwelleth in Mount Zion."

Study Number Thirteen
(Wednesday Afternoon, February 24, 1897)

At the beginning of our work here I felt and expressed myself thus—That I had no heart whatever to go on in simply an ordinary Bible study. You know that in the study of the Word of God there is life and salvation; but just to take an hour and sit here and study certain words, and then go away again, and think no more of it,—I could not endure that. Just as an ordinary study it seemed as though it would be a waste of time, for we had not very much time to spend, and I knew from the beginning we needed something we did not have. I knew that in the book of Hebrews, in the first few chapters especially, there is life and truth, and that in small compass is the special message for this time. We have passed over a certain portion, but I had no heart to go further until we had taken in the truth of what we had studied. Each day it has seemed as though I could not go on; I did not know what there was for us. But each day, as the time came for the lesson, the Lord gave me the message. Well, I am glad we are where we are,—as far as we are. So this afternoon I thought, "What shall we have? What can we do?" And I said to the Lord, "Tell me what the message is, and whether we shall have anything or not." Then came these words, "I will put my trust in him." This is a part of our lesson in Hebrews, the words of Christ. Yesterday we were brought face to face with the fact that the Spirit of God is to do the work, and not we; face to face with the fact that God is waiting to fill his people with the Spirit, that we may accomplish in the earth the work that he designs us to do. There are so many things that we need to know; but I thank the Lord that it need not take us long. But when we receive the Spirit of God, we must receive it understandingly. We are not in the condition that the disciples were when the Spirit was poured out at Pentecost. We are a long way from it. But then I thank the Lord that it need not take us long to get there.

The next summer after the Minneapolis meeting, there was a good brother whom I met for the first time, who, at the close of a meeting, said that he had received help and light; that he had been misinformed, he was sure, in regard to the Minneapolis meeting, and the work which had been done, and he was glad to be able to see some things for himself; glad to see and receive justification by faith. Then thinking how it sounded for a preacher to say that he had learned to accept justification by faith, he added, "Of course, we have always believed in justification by faith, but we have not known what it was." Well, brethren, I have seen a good many hundred people since that time who believed in justification by faith but did not know what it was, and that among Seventh-day Adventists. There are a great many who think they believe it, and who do believe it, who have excepted it to a certain extent only, as a theory. They have taken it as a new article of faith. There is no such thing as a "theory" of justification by faith. It is a fact, that is all; and there are wonderfully few people who allow the fact to get into them for all it is worth.

Now these words that came to me here, "I will put my trust in him," cover the whole ground. That text is everything. Justification by faith is not simply one series or line of truth to be presented to the people. It is the whole truth; it is the third angel's message; there is nothing else. Is there anything else in this world we want except righteousness? Does not that include everything? Because righteousness, we understand is not simply to be a streak in a man's life; it is not simply something for Sabbath. What is righteousness?—Doing right; doing the right thing, instead of the wrong thing—that is righteousness. Not only doing a certain thing right instead of doing it wrong, but always doing the right thing instead of the wrong thing. Is not that simple enough, plain enough as to what righteousness is?

Now, of what is a man's life composed?—His actions. A man's life is composed of his actions; of what he does. If he acts right, he is right. We are not now going into the cause of the thing. We are considering the thing itself; we are not now considering how, why, or whence, righteousness comes, but simply considering the fact and how much it includes. If a man's actions be right, he is a man, a righteous man.

"Let no man deceive you: he that doeth righteousness is righteous."

That is *right*. But if he acts wrong, then he is not right, that's all. These are facts; simple, plain, self-evident truths. They do not need any argument. A man's life is composed of the actions he performs. That is all the Lord brings to the judgment,—the things that men have done. Now to how much of a man's life may the adjectives "righteousness and unrighteousness" apply?—To every act of a man's life. Is that clear? Then righteousness by faith, or in the absence of that, unrighteousness without any help whatever, has to do with a man's whole life; with every act, doesn't it?

(A voice) Yes.

Well, that is righteousness. Is a man a righteous man, and can he be a righteous man, and do right things in some particulars, and then in other particulars go wrong?—No. No; the man is composed of

his acts, and righteousness or unrighteousness has to do with all the acts of man. "He that doeth righteousness is righteous." The righteous man does the right thing under all circumstances of life, and does it in the right way.

Now then, we say we accept the doctrine of righteousness by faith. What does that mean?—Right doing by faith. I know that that language to some seems the wildest nonsense; because the idea of righteousness by faith, of course, is nonsense to some. But many have said that righteousness by faith is a good thing in itself, but it must not be carried to an extreme. That is to say, righteousness by faith is a good thing, but do not be too righteous; do not be too good. Faith in God is a good thing, but do not carry it too far. Don't trust him too much. Now, does this idea of carrying righteousness by faith to an extreme mean anything else than that righteousness is a good thing and faith is a good thing, but that you may have too much of them, and so get on dangerous ground? I am not imagining anything, but simply repeating what I have heard: "Faith is a good thing, but do not carry it to extremes." Brethren, how many of you have supposed that fanaticism is simply an excess of faith? I won't ask you to hold up your hands, but I am sure that I have seen a good many who have supposed that fanaticism was simply an excess of faith; haven't you? Some of them are in the house now. Let me tell you that as long as a man sticks to this word, "I will put my trust in him," so long as he holds to that, you can't make a fanatic out of him, no matter how much you try. He can't be made fanatical. Fanaticism comes from letting go the Word of God, and substituting one's own ideas; but nobody in the world was ever fanatical because he believed the Word of God too much. We need to be so well acquainted with the Lord that we will not be afraid that he can't manage his own business; that he does not know how to do it.

Is it misstating or overstating the ideas that have obtained in the minds of many people among us, to say that they thought that righteousness by faith was a good thing in its place, but that when you come to the steady practical work of the cause, it did not work? Is not that so? That has been a prevailing idea. Now, in the first place we must consider, Do we accept the facts of righteousness by faith? Do we accept the truth that there is no other way of becoming righteous, except by faith? Is there any other way of being righteous?—No. To every act in a man's life the term righteous or unrighteous may be applied; then if a man would be righteous, to how many acts of his life must faith come in as the source?—All of them. Righteousness by faith, then, does not mean that it is something that we will have at some point of our life, the goody goody part, but when we come to business, we want something better.

Faith is not something to be put to one side and sneered at; faith is not imagination; faith is not fancy; faith is not sentimentalism; faith is not guess work; faith is an eternal fact. Therefore if a man be in business, and he would be a righteous man in business, that business, being an act, must be done by faith. Righteousness by faith therefore means, the life of Christ coming in to direct everything that man does, and especially in the cause of God, because as a matter of fact, if we are Christians we do not do anything that is not in the cause of God. As Christians we do not have two parts to our lives; it is all Christian, and if we say we have given ourselves to the cause of God, then we have no business to be in the cause of God a part of the time, and then a little part of the time do something else. Therefore as we are altogether in the cause, in the work, I say righteousness by faith means nothing less than that by faith everything that is done shall be done. It means that the Lord shall act. It means that we shall trust the Lord so that we shall understand; because, "by faith we understand."

The word of God is true. Man is nothing. When God speaks, we are to take his word. It does not make any difference how it comes, when or by whom it comes, we are to say, That is true. Brethren, God has placed authority in the church. That authority is his word illumined by his Holy Spirit. That is the authority. That is the only authority there is. Christ is the leader of the church. "Behold I have given him for a witness to the people, a leader, and a commander to the people." He is the leader; we will follow him. His word is authority, and it alone is authority. When we take the word of God, it does not make any difference if some man in higher position says, "It does not mean that," or, "We cannot apply it; it would do all right in an ideal state, but God must take us where we are, and it cannot be applied here. It cannot be applied there."

With all respect to that man, I do not believe a word of it. I know that the word of God is not visionary, and fanciful, simply dissolving into blue clouds and then into nothing, but God's word is for us to live upon. Brethren, there is that in that word, in the light which God gives to us,—there is that in that word, which will direct us in every thing which we have to do in this world, no matter in what capacity we act. There is instruction in this word for everything that we should do. Numbers who do not believe the truth do not have one iota of effect upon the truth. If ten thousand men do not believe the truth, that does not make it any less the truth. If somebody else cannot see it, that does not make it any the less true that I can see it.

And so God's blessing is upon us, and God is among us; and things that we ought to have known, every one of us, years ago, and have not known, and have deprived ourselves of, and in consequence have been weak, because of our not taking God by his Holy Spirit,—if we only get the key, if we only get the root, if we only get the thing for all that it is worth, we will have eternity for here and everywhere. Dependence upon God is everything. Righteousness by faith is the key that will unlock all these things. So God in his infinite mercy will teach us in a little while—O, how good he is!—that which we have been holding off for years; he will teach us, and we may go forth from this meeting with the power of God to proclaim the truth to the world. So, brethren, let us put our trust in him.

Study Number Fourteen
(Thursday Afternoon, February 25, 1897)

Judging from some of the testimonies I have heard, we are just now where we can begin to study some of the things which we have been passing over. It would, of course, be very pleasant to me if we could pass along, and in the period of time that is allotted to us, go quite through, or nearly through, the book of Hebrews. But it would not be profitable simply for the sake of going over so much ground, if that were all. It would be a grand thing if we were in the condition to take hold and appropriate the matter as we go along. But what we are here for in this Conference is practical results; not for a show at study, but to get something that will be of practical benefit that we can take away with us. Now, you cannot take anything away with you that you do not take inside of you. You cannot take it in your pocket or anywhere outside, but in you. Because the Word of God is life. Who would undertake to go outdoors and gather up a quantity of sunshine so that we could have it in our rooms tonight? But you might just as well think of doing that, as to think of carrying the light of God to people in any other way than in you.

The text we had yesterday was: "I will put my trust in him." Have we learned that lesson yet? I will put my trust in whom?—In God. These are the words of Christ. He says, "I will put my trust in him." In God and in whom else?

(A voice) In Christ.

Yes, but that is the same thing. But the way it usually goes is, I will put my trust in God and—

(Voices) Self.

In God and somebody else, and usually more in man than in God, because we cannot see the Lord. Do you know that heathenism is the most easy and natural thing in the world, and we are not so far from the heathen. People want to trust in something they can see, and they cannot see the Lord, so they do not know about trusting him. They want to trust in something that they can see; so you hear people talking as though it were the height, the extreme height of trust in the Lord, when we cannot see what he is doing. What wonderful trust! Somebody wants to borrow some money of me, and I let him have it. I trust him with it, but I keep watch of him. He goes down the walk, I follow him. What are you doing?—I am trusting that man. He turns a corner; I follow him. What are you doing?—I am trusting him. He goes into a house; I go as far as I can, and watch the door. What are you doing?—I am trusting that man where I can't see him. That is no trust; it is distrust and suspicion. It is an insult to him; but no one thinks of treating a man in such a way. It is only God whom they feel free to insult, because they cannot see the Lord, and he does not resent their treatment as men would.

I say we have a good deal to learn in that text, "I will put my trust in him." What are the grounds of our putting our trust in the Lord? If you are going to trust your money to any man, you inquire something about his financial standing. You wish to know in regard to his honesty. You must have some grounds for trusting him. Now what ground have we for putting our trust in the Lord?—He is strong, he is wise, he is stronger than we are, and he knows more than we do. He is almighty and all wise. How many believe that the Lord knows more than they do? We tell the Lord that we cannot do anything without him, and then go right on doing things without him. We have taken as an article of our creed, that without the Lord we cannot do anything. We all profess to believe that without the Lord we cannot do anything, and then we go right along and begin figuring and planning without taking the Lord into the account at all. Now, how much sense is there in that?

We have a lesson of trust in the fiftieth chapter of Isaiah. To show who it is that is speaking, so we will have no difficulty on that question, read the sixth verse: "I gave my back to the smiters, and my cheeks to them that plucked off the hair: I hid not my face from shame and speaking." Who is speaking?—It is Christ. Now come back to the fourth verse and onward:—

The Lord God hath given me the tongue of the learned, that I should know how to speak a word in season to him that is weary: he wakeneth morning by morning, he wakeneth mine ear to hear as the learned.

The Lord God hath opened mine ear, and I was not rebellious, neither turned away back. I gave my back to the smiters, and my cheeks to them that plucked off the hair: I hid not my face from shame and spitting.

For the Lord God will help me; therefore shall I not be confounded; therefore have I set my face like a flint, and I know that I shall not be ashamed. He is near that justifieth me; who will contend with me? let us stand together: who is mine adversary? let him come near to me. Behold, the Lord God will help me; who is he that shall condemn me? lo, they all shall wax old as a garment; the moth shall eat them up.

Who is among you that feareth the Lord, that obeyeth the voice of his servant, that walketh in darkness and hath no light? let him trust in the name of the Lord, and stay upon his God. Behold, all ye that kindle a fire, that compass yourselves about with sparks: walk in the light of your fire, and in the sparks that ye have kindled. This shall ye have of mine hand; ye shall lie down in sorrow.

The tenth verse tells when to trust, and it is the only time when we can trust in the Lord. It is when we cannot see; and how much of the Lord's way, how much of the Lord can we see any time?—Nothing. Clouds and darkness are round about him, but here we have the Lord, and we are to trust in him. The Lord hath given me the tongue of the learned, that I should know how to speak the right thing at the right time: "The Lord hath opened mine ear, and I was not rebellious, neither turned away back." Notice the simple statement in Psalm 40:6–9:—

> Sacrifice and offering thou didst not desire; mine ears hast thou opened; burnt offering and sin offering hast thou not required. Then said I, Lo, I come: in the volume of the book it is written of me, I delight to do thy will, O my God, yea, thy law is within my heart. I have preached righteousness in the great congregation: lo, I have not refrained my lips, O Lord, thou knowest.

Now turn to the book of Luke. The second chapter tells of the birth of Christ, the presentation in the temple, the return to Nazareth, of course after they had been in Egypt. "And the child grew, and waxed strong in spirit, filled with wisdom." Or, literally, "becoming filled with wisdom." The child grew, and waxed strong in spirit, becoming filled with wisdom. Now in the remaining part of the chapter we have that wonderful story of the trip to Jerusalem, and of Jesus talking with the doctors in the temple. We see in the pictures always, "Jesus disputing with the doctors," which shows that people who make pictures do not always know the Bible, because we have no record of his disputing, and it would have been most unseemly in a boy of twelve. He was there to improve every opportunity he could to learn something; but, although he was not there as a teacher, yet he could teach the doctors something, and he did that in the questions he asked, and in his answers. Do you suppose, can you suppose, that in the attitude of Jesus there in the temple, when twelve years of age, there was anything out of place, out of keeping with the proper conduct of a child twelve years old to those who were aged? anything immodest, or forward, or assuming, or bold in his character?—No. Just as a little boy he wandered in where the law was being taught, because his tastes led that way. They wondered at the answers he gave them, so clear, so deep, and they wondered that the questions he asked them opened up things even to their minds. But yet there was nothing that was not perfectly in keeping with the actions of a proper child, twelve years old.

W. W. Prescott.—I was very much interested in a statement I recently saw in the "Life of Christ," which is soon to appear; it is that those doctors thought, "What a young man that would be, if we could only instruct him right." What a man we could make of him.

Now the last verse: Jesus increased in wisdom and age, or maturity, and in favor with God and man. Think a little about the wisdom of Jesus. We do not half appreciate it. You remember that he had to meet those same doctors, if not, others fully as wise, all his life. He was forced to meet them, because they put themselves on his track; they were the scribes, the Pharisees, the Sadducees, the educated class of the Jews. The Jews as a people were not ignorant. The Jewish people of that day were permeated with Greek literature and philosophy, and all the wisdom of the Greeks. Greek was commonly used among them. Those doctors were the most polished and cultured of the people; they spent their lives in sharpening their wits by considering hard problems and perplexing questions.

These men set themselves to work to entrap this young man who was bold enough to go around teaching the people, without having gone through their curriculum. How many times did they do it? How many times did they catch him?—Not once. They asked him a good many hard questions, and they thought they had cornered him; but did they do it? You and I would give a good deal to be able to act as wisely as Jesus did. Every time he knew the right thing to say, and the right thing to do, and when not to say anything. Was there a person in the world who was as keen of intellect, who knew just how to meet every emergency as did Jesus? You know he was wiser than Solomon. How did he get that wisdom?—It was by the Spirit of God. The Spirit of God made him of quick understanding in the fear of the Lord. But at what time in his life did this wonderful wisdom come to him? Was it as a revelation in a vision that it came to him?—No; the child grew and increased in wisdom. Was there any wisdom in Jesus—who never made a mistake, to whom the most abstruse questions were referred,—was there any wisdom in Jesus that might not be in other people?—No; for he himself is made unto us wisdom. He was always ready. When the time came that called for wisdom, the wisdom was there. Now, how did he get that wisdom, how did it come to him?

(A voice) It was intuition.

Then he was not like us at all. We read that "it behooved him to be made in all things like unto his brethren;" that is, in every particular. We do not want to put the Lord off away from us, but he is one of us. "I have exalted one chosen out of the people." "Behold, I will raise up one from among the brethren." He was one of the people, one of the common people, just an ordinary laboring man. How did he come by his wisdom? Here is the statement given in the thirteenth verse that answers the question, "I will put my trust in him." Now what did he study that gave him this wonderful insight into men, their character, and his knowledge of men's needs, and which enabled him to know how not simply to answer questions, but how to teach the people?—He studied God's Word. "I delight to do thy law, O my God." "Yea, thy law is within my heart." There you have it. He was wholly given to the Lord, knowing that there is no other use for man in this world but to serve the Lord. That is the business of life—to please the Lord. Hearken as we read in the fiftieth chapter of Isaiah:—

"The Lord God hath given me the tongue of the learned, that I should know how to speak a word in season to him that is weary; he wakeneth morning by morning, he wakeneth mine ear to hear as the learned."

Then he kept learning something day by day. He increased, he studied the Word, and submitted to the Spirit; that was all. Turn to Prov. 1:23: "Turn ye at my reproof." I am thankful to God for the indication of the willingness of this delegation, of this body of delegates, to comply with these words.

(Audience) Amen.

That is good. But, brethren, I am wonderfully afraid that you are not going much further than that. This is only the first part. "Turn ye." I have wondered today how much more we know today, how much more wisdom we have, than day before yesterday. What did we get yesterday?

(A voice) Something of the Lord's will.

(Another voice) Reproof.

Yes, we received many statements as to what mistakes have been made, and wrong courses that have been taken. That was the principal thing. It was seen that in many things we had been wholly wrong. Now, does a man's acknowledgment that he has made a mistake give him wisdom, so that he will not make a mistake again?—No. That is where we are now. Day before yesterday, night before last, all the committees felt that they had come to a place where they did not know what to do; where they said, "We cannot go on any further." Yesterday we had the Testimonies read that told us about the wrong, in this or in that part of the cause, wrong upon this or that line of working; and we said, "That is so, Lord; that is good." The Lord showed that he responded to that. Now what? We have had the experience, and now we are ready to go on, because we know all about it. The Testimony has told us about it; it has said we have done wrong, and we have acknowledged it, and now we can go on—go on and do what?—The same things over again; that is all. Although you have acknowledged your wrong, what warrant have any of you that you will not do the same thing again? Who in the first place went wrong intentionally?—Nobody intended to do so. Everybody thought he was doing the right thing. If you had known that you were going wrong, would you have done it?—Certainly not. You have all been honest and sincere, and wanted to do the work of the Lord in the best manner possible. And you do not want to do right now, perhaps, any more than you wanted to do right then. You are just as anxious to do right now as then, and you were just as anxious then as now. But now it is pointed out to you; you made mistakes and went wrong; and you say, "Yes." Now we acknowledge the mistakes, and go ahead, and do what?—Go ahead and make another record of mistakes, and come up again where we will have testimonies, and we will have to say again, "The thing is all wrong," and then go over it all again. What shall we do?

(A voice) Seek God for wisdom.

Well, now, we will say, "We won't do that any more. We see now that we have been following the wrong plan. There are some defects in our organization. We have not managed it all right. That has brought these things about. Now we will divide up a little differently, we will reapportion out districts, so as to avoid putting so much responsibility upon a few men. We will put the responsibility on more men, so we won't do that as before." Now, brethren, I must fear that we are deliberately planning, without intention, of course, to go ahead and make not the same mistakes as before, in the same way, but to make some worse ones in a different way. What warrant have you that you won't do that?

(A voice) Trust in the Lord, and expect that he will guide us.

That is very good, but how often we deceive ourselves. We think we are trusting in the Lord when we bow down and pray to the Lord before our committee meetings, and then get up and try to scheme and guess, to cut and try, and figure; and do not know. The Lord did not do that way. The Lord knew what he was doing. How did he know? He did not make these mistakes; and the Lord has given us these reproofs for a purpose, in order that we may not make any more mistakes. Notice: "Turn ye at my reproof." He has called attention, and everybody has turned. He said, "Halt," and we stopped. That is good. We turned to hear what he had to say. Now what is the next?—"I will pour out my Spirit unto you, I will make known my words unto you." That is the next thing. To accept this which has been given, to receive the reproof of the Lord, to accept it—that is a great deal. But what warrant has any man, after having accepted that reproof, that he won't go ahead and make the same mistakes in some other way?—No warrant whatever; not in the least.

Question.—Will not God guide us?

Answer.—If we let him; but we won't let him.

Question.—Is not the promise based upon the fact that we turn at his reproof?

Answer.—Yes, but we must allow him to fulfill that promise in us. "I will pour out my Spirit unto you." Have we had that result?—No; we have not had that yet. We get in such a hurry that we run ahead of the Lord. We play the part of Joab's servant. Where is your message?—"O, I haven't any, but let me run." And so we run, and run, in vain. Now the Lord studied the Word, and from the Word of God, Jesus got all the wisdom he ever had. How much more do you and I desire to know than he knew? In what lines was he deficient that we want to perfect ourselves in? In what lines was he deficient that we want to be proficient in? He had at least seventy men under him whose work he had to direct; so he knew something about running a conference. He had more preachers under him than any presidents of conferences that you know of. So he could give instruction in that line. Where did he get it from?—"O, he looked up the Jewish records, and saw how they did the work, and then modeled his plans upon that;"—did he? "He took the Methodist Discipline, and looked at the mission boards of other denominations, and saw how they worked, and then modeled his plans after that." Where did he get his wisdom?—Out of the Word of the Lord, didn't he? from God's Word, and that alone with the enlightenment of the Holy Spirit.

He was not rebellious, did not turn back; but when the Word came, he did not pick it to pieces to subject it to the trial of his own intellect, but he took it in, and let that enlarge his intellect. That is the way we want to take the Word—instead of subjecting the Word, God's Word, and his Spirit and teaching, to our intellect and reason, we must take it in. What good does it do us then? It will enlarge our capacity and comprehension.

Now somebody will say, "What is your plan of work? What changes shall be made in our organization?—I do not know anything about that. But here is something I do know: *I know where wisdom is to be obtained*. And now, whatever we may say about school work, or anything of that kind (it all comes to the same thing),—whatever we say about any other kind of work, certainly if we find any wisdom whatever in the Word, it ought to be upon how to carry on the work of the Lord. If you cannot find out how to carry on the work of the Lord, in the Bible, what can you expect to find?

Don't you suppose we can find in the Bible all we need for carrying the work of the Lord on earth? But that is about the last place one thinks of looking, isn't it? You say, "I don't see anything in here about electing a president of a Conference. The Lord leaves that to human agents. The Lord has not gone into details; he has left man to carry out details." The attention of the Lord is not so occupied that he cannot give attention to details. That is one of the things we have been studying—the Lord in creation, in every single thing; the Lord personally caring for every part of his universe. Every detail in the universe has his personal supervision.

(A voice) Do you think that God bothers himself about all these things?

O, no; not a bit of it. God is so great that he can give attention to all these things, and not be bothered at all. That is God.

Now I will put my trust in him. The lesson to be learned, and the whole truth of the third angel's message, the gospel in a nutshell, is simply in this—*that God is everything, and man is nothing*.

As compared with God, we are vanity, nothing, and even less than nothing. Men of low degree are vanity, and men of high degree are a lie. Men of low degree are only vanity, but men of high degree are a lie because they profess to be something when they too are only vanity. Now, if man is nothing but ignorance, and God is everything, all wise, would it be wise to leave God out, and let man take care of the details? If God knows everything, and man does not know anything, it would be wisdom to let God give directions in everything. If he is all wisdom, what is to hinder him from going into details? If he knows it all, what is to hinder him from going to the whole length, and showing man how to do all the work?

But now I imagine that I hear some one remarking that this is discouraging. You are putting us right where we were before.

Well, it did not seem discouraging yesterday, did it? Was anything said yesterday to discourage any body?—No. The Lord does not utter a discouraging word to a single soul. No, "he shall not fail, nor be discouraged until he have set judgment in the earth." Then what is the use of our being discouraged? He does not talk discouragement to anybody. "But he says some pretty hard things."

Yes; but it is not to discourage us. When the Lord sends reproof, who brings it?

(A voice) The Holy Spirit.

What is his name, who is he?

(A voice) Comforter.

Comforter; then the reproof is the very first step in comfort. When he comes, he will convince the world of sin, and of righteousness. Good! Let us take the whole thing. Let us take whatever the Spirit has to give to us. What does the Spirit give? "The Spirit searcheth all things, yea, the deep things of God." "O the depths and the riches both of the wisdom and knowledge of God."

The whole work is saving souls. I am not going to find any fault or criticize a single thing that exists in the work. I am content, perfectly content, that everything, every organization, be just as it is. There are certain things that we have set in operation, presumably for the purpose of assisting in the work of the Lord, in forwarding the message, in the work of saving souls. Now when we look back over what we have done, can we flatter ourselves very much with the progress we have made? Has it been a brilliant success? What we heard yesterday certainly will keep us from boasting very much. Now, having tried to work in our own way, would it not be fair to give at least a just trial to the Lord's way.

Here is a lily growing. That is the standard given for us. "Consider the lily." The lily starts out in the spring. It is going to make a considerable growth this year; but before it can think of growing at all, it will stop and lay plans for the summer's growth, and measure just exactly how much it is going to grow, and what it is going to be. It must devise and measure it all out; have a plan laid out. If it did that, it would never grow. What is the proper size and shape of a tree? How high must a tree be? how great must be its circumference? what its diameter? how high from the ground must the first branch put forth? how far apart must each branch be? how many branches must it have? and how many leaves must each branch bear? O, that depends upon the tree. And for that matter, you cannot fix it, because it does not stop growing. It keeps growing as long as it lives. Now, the Lord says that his people shall be trees of righteousness, and Christ was one of the model trees. How was it with the model tree? He kept growing and increasing in stature, and learning something, not because that is the way somebody else had done, but because God was in him.

Brethren, we have got only a little glimmer of light. The light that God has for us would dazzle our eyes if he would give it to us now, because we have accustomed ourselves to so much darkness. By and by the light will shine from heaven in such a way that people who have not been used to the light, will run and hide in holes, and who here is going to do that? If we do not get our eyes opened pretty soon, so that we can take the light a little faster than we have been taking it, it may be that some of us who are here will hide in holes when the Lord shines forth.

Question.—Are we to understand that Christ's knowledge was acquired?

Most certainly it was. There was no other way. He was not born with wisdom. But we have in the first chapter of 1 Corinthians this statement: "The foolishness of God is wiser than men, and the weakness of God is stronger than men." Where can you find anything more foolish and helpless than a little baby? In the twenty-first Psalm we read that Christ was cast upon the Lord from his mother's womb. There God manifested what he could do. The one thing we want to learn is, "I will put my trust in him." Learn to trust the Lord, for the Lord knows more about anything than we know. Whatever we know about anything in the world, the Lord knows more about it than we do.

The one thing that rests upon my mind is, Are we going to become acquainted with the Lord, and get in touch with him, so that we can know when he speaks, and talk with him day by day, so that we shall know what to do and how to do it? and if we are not, what in the world is going to hinder us from making the mistakes we have been making all these years? It does not make any difference how sorry we are for a thing. That does no good unless we go farther. That is good of itself, the right kind of sorrow that works repentance. The thing for us now to say is, Lord, we accept the reproof. Pour out thy Spirit upon us. Give to us the enlightenment of thy Spirit. I was reading yesterday a statement that it is for the people of God now to be gathering together, and seeking the Lord for the outpouring and the filling of his Holy Spirit. That is what we need for the work. And when we have the Holy Spirit's enlightenment, then we will know the Lord day by day. He will open our eyes. He will talk with us, and these things that are wrong will drop away. The work of the Lord is to build up. We do not have to set ourselves to tearing anything down, but just let the Lord fill us with the Spirit,—the spirit of wisdom and of understanding, the spirit of counsel and of knowledge and of the fear of the Lord, which will make us of quick understanding in the fear of the Lord. Then whatever we have that is right, will go right along with us; and whatever we have that is unnecessary and useless, will drop off. There is one thing, brethren, we want to do here, and that is to say, Lord we take these reproofs, and we are waiting to be filled with thy Holy Spirit; and then expect that we shall have his words made known unto us, and we will find that there is light. But then do not think that there is the place to stop. There is no stopping-place. People get a little light, and then the first thing they know they are troubled because they are expected to get some more light. They do not like to be troubled with getting accustomed to more light. They want a rule laid down, so that they will know just the thing that they are to say and teach. Well, the only rule is progression, eternal progression. The path is as the shining light which shineth more and more unto the perfect day. And when that perfect day dawns our eyes will be so accustomed to seeing the light of the Lord, that we can see the full and unveiled glory of the Lord, and our eyes will not be dimmed.

Study Number Fifteen
(Friday Afternoon, February 26, 1897)

We may begin here as though we were leaving off at the close of the hour. If any one has any questions to ask, perhaps it would be better for them to be given now. So if there are any practical questions upon any of these points we have been considering—practical questions, not speculations—we should be glad to consider them.

Elder Lane.—I was asked yesterday if I thought you were teaching that although we lived very near to God, and had much of his blessing, we would ever come to understand the minds and very motives as Christ did. This was a question which resulted from the statement you made that Christ had no more than we may have. It says in regard to him that he knew what was in man. So if we have enough faith, can we reach that same point?

Twelfth chapter of 1Corinthians. I do not know anything, I have no opinion whatever, except what I read; and all can know what is written just as well as I.

Wherefore I give you to understand, that no man speaking by the Spirit of God calleth Jesus accursed; and that no man can say that Jesus is the Lord, but by the Holy Ghost. Now there are diversities of gifts, but the same Spirit. And there are differences of administrations, but the same Lord. And there are diversities of operations, but it is the same God which worketh all in all. But the manifestation of the Spirit is given to every man to profit withal. For to one is given by the Spirit the word of wisdom; to another the word of knowledge by the same Spirit; to another faith by the same Spirit; to another the gifts of healing by the same Spirit; to another the working of miracles; to another prophecy; to another discerning of spirits; to another divers kinds of tongues; to another the interpretation of tongues: but all these worketh that one and the selfsame Spirit, dividing to every man severally as he will.

But to every one the Spirit is given to profit withal. Therefore when the people of God come to be the people of God indeed,—come to give up their own way, their own devices, their own schemes, for the Lord himself to be their wisdom, God himself to be in them by his Spirit, in his fullness,—then the gifts of the Spirit will be in the church because every living soul will have some gift of the Spirit. The Spirit divides to every man severally as he will. Discerning of spirits is one of these. I know of but one man in the world since the time of Christ, who had all the gifts of the Spirit at one time. That was the apostle Paul; he had the whole series, an apostle, a teacher, an evangelist, a prophet, a discerner of spirits, talking with tongues, interpretation of tongues, the gift of miracles, the gift of healing—all found in that one man. I never read of another man who had such an abundance of gifts. But God takes everybody, every individual, and gives to every one his work. He gives to every man according to his several ability, according to the work God designs he shall do. The fullness of the Spirit in him will make him competent for that work. God will give to every soul just the gifts that are needed for every occasion.

We do not need to explain as to the operation of the Spirit. The essential thing for us is the acceptance of the Spirit. Then whatever the Spirit is pleased to work in us, we will give God the glory. But we will not choose. We have the statement, "As he is, so are we in this world." "God was in Christ, reconciling the world unto himself." He has put into us that same word of reconciliation. "So then we are ambassadors for God, as though God did beseech you by us," in his stead. The same work, you see, the very same work is given to us, that was given to Christ: "As my Father hath sent me, even so send I you." To fit him for his work, "in him dwelt all the fullness of the Godhead." So the inspired prayer of the disciple for us is,—

That he would grant you, according to the riches of his glory, to be strengthened with might by his Spirit in the inner man; that Christ may dwell in your hearts by faith: that ye, being rooted and grounded in love, may be able to comprehend with all saints what is the breadth, and length, and depth, and height; and to know the love of Christ, which passeth knowledge, that ye might be filled with all the fullness of God.

There is no difference; the same things are given to us, that were given to Jesus, for we are joint heirs with him. That is not lowering Christ. It is not depreciating Christ, but it is the Spirit endeavoring to give us a conception of the wonderful height to which God lifts man. The Spirit desires that the eyes of your understanding may be enlightened; that ye may know what is the hope of his calling, and what the riches of the glory of his inheritance in the saints, and what is the exceeding greatness of his power to us-ward who believe. He wants us to see and know these things. Is there another question?

(A voice) How could Jesus trust in God when he was a very small child, if all the wisdom he had was acquired?

I cannot explain it; it is enough for me to know that he did. Of course the question hinges on that word if—if all the wisdom he has was acquired.

Elder Fifield.—It seems to me that some of the most perfect trust there is, is that of the child. The Bible says, Except ye be converted, and become as little children.

Of course children trust. But we get the idea that because children are small, and do not bother themselves about things as we do, they do not trust, when they have a great deal more than we do. Men build up doubt by their vain reasonings and philosophies only to knock it down again; but the child is not so foolish as to build up a great pile of stuff that he has to knock down again.

But to return to that point, as to Jesus' acquiring knowledge. It is a vital one, just as any other. On that depends whether we are going to get all the benefit of Christ, or whether we are going to dig a ditch and make a separation. Now, if he was such a monstrosity that as a child he had enough knowledge to fit out a full-grown man, what likeness is there between him and us? What benefit can we get from his experience? What a big advantage he had over us then. Could I get any benefit from his experience in such a case?—No; it would simply be discouraging. But it says that he was tempted in all points like as we are. "It behooved him in all things to be made like unto his brethren." There is the benefit, the advantage.

Elder Jones suggests that the words in Ps.22:9,10, make it plain. The Lord kept him as a child, as a youth, and as a man; and he will do the same thing for us, if we put our trust in him.

Now take the case of Solomon, who, according to the Bible, was the wisest man that the world ever saw. There was none like him before or after, and all the world came to see the wisdom of Solomon. How did he get his wisdom?—God gave it to him? Did he go to bed one night, and wake up the next morning a wise man? He himself has told us how he got his wisdom, and how we may get it. It is true that he sought the Lord. The Lord said, What will you have? He said, I will have wisdom. The Lord says to us, What will you have? We desire wisdom, too. We are in continual need of wisdom about something or other. How shall we get it?—"If any man lack wisdom, let him ask of God who giveth to all liberally, and upbraideth not, and it shall be given him." But let him be watchful about one thing. Let him ask in faith. How does faith come?—By hearing. Hearing what?—The Word of God. Let him ask, then, according to the Word of God. If he asks according to the Word of God, there is no doubt about his getting wisdom. Solomon asked for wisdom, and he got it. Turn to the second chapter of Proverbs, and we shall find out how he got it. There is only one way. The old proverb used to be that there is no royal way to knowledge. But there is. That is the only way there is to learn. Solomon was a king and he has given us the royal way to wisdom. And this is not simply Solomon's opinion. It is the Spirit of God speaking through Solomon, and what the Spirit of God spoke to Solomon, he speaks to us. Let us read it:—

My son, if thou wilt receive my words, and hide my commandments with thee; so that thou incline thine ear unto wisdom, and apply thine heart to understanding; yea, if thou criest after knowledge, and liftest up thy voice for understanding; if thou seekest her as silver, and searchest for her as for hid treasures; then shalt thou understand the fear of the Lord, and find the knowledge of God. For the Lord giveth wisdom: out of his mouth cometh knowledge and understanding. He layeth up sound wisdom for the righteous: he is a buckler to them that walk uprightly. He keepeth the paths of judgment, and preserveth the way of his saints. Then shalt thou understand righteousness, and judgment, and equity; yea every good path.

How did Solomon get his understanding?—He dug for it. He cried for it day and night. That is the way men seek silver and gold. That is the way the millionaires get their money. They put their minds on that one thing to the exclusion of every other thing day and night, because they would rather have money than anything else. Now, we would rather have wisdom than anything else, because the wisdom of God is salvation, and the salvation of God is everything. We have the key to the whole universe then. Solomon studied. He asked the Lord, and then studied, and the Lord gave him light. He studied God's Word, "for the Lord giveth wisdom, out of his mouth cometh understanding." So Solomon got his wisdom from the Word of God, and he did not have nearly so much of the written word as we have. But there was not another thing that Solomon had to make him the wisest man the world ever saw. Do you believe it? It was just by the study of the Word of the Lord.

Some of you do not believe it, because you have read the Old Testament through, and you did not find very much in it. I have traveled across Nevada and Colorado, and I never saw any silver or gold in either State. Shall I say that I do not believe there is any gold or silver in these States because I never saw any there? But it is there nevertheless.

I was not looking for it when I was there, and did not dig for it. Other men have found lots of it there. Some men may say that they see wisdom in the Bible, but only in certain directions; it does not tell a man how he ought to do in a Conference. It does not tell a man how he ought to do in his own affairs. How do you know it does not? You may say you have not found it there. It is one thing to say it is not there, and another to say you have not found it; because it has been found. Solomon found it there. And the Lord found it there, because he was greater than Solomon. Jesus was wiser than Solomon, and we have access to the same source of instruction that Solomon had.

The question will come, How shall we know when we get the truth, that it is the truth? How shall we know we have the right way. I will tell you how you cannot know: if you use your mind to speculate, and try to reason things out. You get hold of some subject, some idea, then take that and try to drive it through the Bible, and use one text here, and another text there, and another text elsewhere, that will fit,—while you may have a pretty good theory, you cannot *know* anything about whether you are right or not. Of course you cannot. You will always be in doubt. The most you will be able to say is that according to your best judgment so and so is the truth. That is not studying the Bible at all. That is studying yourself, and trying to get the Bible to agree with you. It is another thing from studying the Bible. The same doubt will also always be in your minds when you take truth at second hand. The Lord says, Dig, just as you would for treasure. Take the Word, and look at it, and delve into it, until its truths are imprinted in your mind. And let them be turning over and over and over, just keeping them until they are digested and assimilated, and we get the good that there is in them. And then the light comes. It is life and you see it. Now, from my own experience I tell you that is the only way to learn anything of the Bible.

Elder G. F. Watson.—Do you understand that we should not study by subjects?

You cannot study the Bible that way. Nobody ever studies the Bible by subjects. That is not studying the Bible at all. You study the Bible itself, without reference to subjects, and then when a man asks you a question on any subject you are ready, no matter where he strikes you; you fall upon your feet every time. It makes no difference where you start in, it is there, and you see it. Now, when you take a portion of Scripture, read it and reread it, keeping your mind fixed upon it as though you would see to the bottom of it,—why, it is just wonderful. I can say for myself, that I do not deserve any credit for anything I know, because I have not obtained it by any shrewdness I have in studying things out. I simply take a scripture and look at it, and look at it. I want to know what it says, and that is all, without any speculation; and I will not allow myself to think, even myself by myself, one hair's breadth from what the Bible says. I have not any curiosity to speculate about the Bible; my curiosity is just all in abeyance. The trouble is, we go a little way in the Word, and then start off on a speculation, going on nothing, wondering about this, and building up this theory and that theory; but we have no business to do that. It is not fair to treat ourselves or anybody else that way. I simply keep looking and looking, and it comes. Now, can a man know a thing that he sees? If the window is open here, and we look out, can we tell what we see?

We look out here, and we see the sun shining; and we look out on the other side, and we see the sun itself. Then do we call two or three of the brethren, and say, Now, I want to be sure that I am right on this? I see something there; is that light? or is it not light? I want to be sure. The window is open, and I ask, Is that light? or is that not light? What would you think was the matter with me?—You would think I was blind. We want to be able to know light when we see it. And it certainly ought not to be a difficult thing for one to be able to do that. I would not give a farthing if every one in this house should go with me out into the street, and tell me the sun is shining. That would not help me one bit. You think I am wonderfully conceited, don't you, because I can tell when the sun is shining? Well, I have fairly good eyesight, and what I see I know.

Now, when we get acquainted with the Lord, we know the light, and we do not need to have somebody to tell us that it is light. Every one of us has to have that knowledge for himself, so that he can know it for himself; and he does not need to have anybody to tell him about it. We have that statement in 1 John 2:20: "Ye have an unction from the Holy One." Have we? Settle that point. "And know all things." How can that be?—Because just as it is told in the fourteenth chapter of John, "The Comforter which is the Holy Ghost, whom the Father will send in my name, he will teach you all things." He will not teach us anything wrong. He will lead us into all truth. How much will there be that we need to know that we cannot have, and cannot find out? Now 1 John 2:27:—

> But the anointing which ye have received of him abideth in you, and ye need not that any man teach you: but as the same anointing teacheth you of all things, and is truth, and is no lie, and even as it hath taught you, ye shall abide in him.

Whoever receives any truth, no matter how true it is, from a man, and recognizes that as coming from a man, has not the truth at all. Whoever will quote a man, when he is trying to teach somebody,—well he is not teaching with authority. He does not know what he is trying to teach, and cannot expect that the people will. The man who knows the truth teaches as though there was not another man on earth who believed it. He knows it so thoroughly that any number of men in this world denying it would not have the least effect upon him.

Elder Kauble.—Is it not just as possible for a man to be positive that he sees light when he does not see it, as for a man to be positive that he sees light when he does see it?

No; it is impossible. A man cannot be sure of a thing that is not so. A man may be deceived, but we have no business to be deceived. What in the world are we in the world for as teachers, if we do not see and know the truth? What business have we to go out and teach somebody else what we do not absolutely know? How dare we do it, and thus run the risk of leading him astray?

Question.—Was not Paul just as positive when he went about persecuting the disciples, that he was doing God's service, as he was after he was converted?

No; he was kicking against the pricks.

Elder Kauble.—I read in the Testimonies that we ought not to teach new doctrines until after counseling with the leading brethren. The question comes, Are we to take our own individual judgment as to what is light?

No; we are not to take our own individual judgment about anything. Cursed is the man that trusteth in man. There is nothing so accursed as for a man to trust in himself. We have the mind of the Spirit to depend on, instead of our own. That statement in the

Testimonies is needed, but we need not be worried over it. Did you ever meet a man, and he would say, I have a new sermon, a new point, some new light. He tells you about it, and says, What do you think about this. He does not mean, of course, to ask your advice, but only to get your assent to his theory, so that he will feel more secure. I will tell you that in all my experience I have never seen anything in that way. In all my experience in the truth I have never yet found a new point, or gone to any one and said, I have a new point; because I never tried to get out anything new. I have not the slightest sympathy with anybody that goes about to get out new theories. Such a one could be in better business than that.

Elder Ballenger.—Are we not commanded to get things new and old out of the storehouse?

That is all right; I did not say that I do not get things new, for I am getting such things all the time. But we do not get new things by jerks. We are not studying to find something to unload on somebody else, or to arouse the anxiety of the congregation with the thought that they are going to get something that will tickle them, something that will create a sensation, that will be startlingly new, and that nobody ever thought of before. Such a man always does harm, even though there be some truth in that which he has. Truth is always the same, the old, old story, and yet it is always new. It is life, new life; it is the old thing always brightening up. It is eternal life. We live in eternity, if we are the Lord's. He has given us eternal life, the power of the world to come. And the one characteristic, the chief characteristic of it is, that it is always fresh. The earth made new will be just as new after ten thousand years, as the first day. The man who reads a text of scripture before a congregation, and does not every time he reads that text learn something new from it, has not his eyes upon God. It is not something that you can sit down and jot down with the pen and ink; it simply comes. The new things that come to me are not the things that I keep a memorandum of, so that I can go about and say, Here I have another new thought. Indeed, the man that gets so little light that he can keep a memorandum of it, does not get enough to do him much good. It just keeps coming, coming, coming, like the rising of the sun. You cannot mark it. You cannot make two successive marks indicating the rising sun's position in the heavens. When you make the second, it is not there. It is rising. It is higher, continually higher. So is the light from the Sun of Righteousness. Light is life, and life is growth, continual growth.

(A voice) Such a man is going on and on; he is growing. "The path of the just is as a shining light, that shineth more and more unto the perfect day."

Why, brethren, if we had to meet together to decide upon every ray of light that God gives, we should have to be in General Conference all the year around. Light is coming all the time. A man cannot put his hand out and mark it. You cannot, no man in this world can write out a synopsis of faith, and tell the truth. You cannot get at it in that way. Truth is from God, and must be drank in as he has given it. A man is not to go around conscious of how much he knows. There is only one help to Bible study, and that is the Spirit of God.

Question.—Do we understand that receiving the Word of God is receiving the Spirit of God?

Yes, if you receive the Word of God indeed, because it is a living thing; it is the bread of life. If you take it as written by some other man, it is not Spirit at all. But if you take it as the living Word, spoken by God himself, then it is life.

But, as I was saying, we are not to go around burdened with a sense of what we know. Why, brethren, when the apostles received the Spirit of God, do you suppose they went around all the time burdened with the consciousness of power? Christ said to them, Ye shall receive power after that the Holy Ghost is come upon you; but do you suppose they went about conscious of that power?—No; they were simply ordinary men the same as before, without any consciousness of power; but when the occasion for a certain thing arose, being always yielded to the Spirit, they were ready for the occasion.

Brethren, we need to study the Bible; stop fooling with it; stop using it as a plaything; begin to study it, and believe there is something in it. There is more in it than you have any idea of. There is everything in it.

We are studying the question, "I will put my trust in him." We have seen justification by faith is the bottom and the substance of everything. See here, as we saw in what we read the other day, the failure to receive—not simply to assent to, but to receive—righteousness by faith is the cause of all these complications and these difficulties that have arisen. Do you see the point? Does that teach you anything? Does that not teach this, that if we all accepted righteousness by faith, and all that is in it,—because that means eternity of progress,—if we received it into our lives, we should know just how to do in everything? because it would open up the whole Bible to us, and then we would be saved all these difficulties, and all the snarls that we get into, and not have to spend so much time getting out. The trouble with many people is, trusting in the Lord makes them think, and it is hard work to think, and so they would rather trust in themselves. Now, that seems like a paradox. A great many people think that the worker who trusts in the Lord, and who preaches by faith, is the man who doesn't think. How many times, as I have tried to impress upon the ministers that they should depend upon the Lord for their preaching just as much as they do for their living right, have I heard the objection raised, "We must not be haphazard; we must not go at random; we must not depend upon the spur of the moment, and go and give whatever we happen to have in our minds."

The testimonies say all that. But who said that depending upon the Lord was going at haphazard? You might as well say that the man who trusts in the Lord, to be kept from sin, is going in an utterly reckless, foolish way. It does look foolish to the man who doesn't know anything about it. And I know how foolish it used to seem to me, how absurd, to think that man, by believing, could be protected from doing a wrong thing. But I know it now, and there is no foolishness in it. There is no going at random about it, for it holds a man right to the Rock all the time; and the man who throws himself into the hands of the Lord, that he will preach by faith—do you suppose he isn't going to think and study? The reason why so many people do not trust the Lord is because it requires so much thinking; when instead of that they can just take a little time, when they feel well, and think for an hour or two, and work out a subject to their satisfaction, and they are forever free from thinking on that subject. Then when they get ready to preach, they can get out their notes, and all the time they know exactly how much they know, because they have it in their pocket. But, brethren, you cannot carry the Word of God in that way. You cannot carry the Word of God in your pocket. You have to carry it inside of your own heart. It has got to be a part of yourself. And as you go along, you may be unconscious that you know anything about a certain thing—the whole thing is gone from your mind, because you don't need to use it then, and some brother comes along and says, "What is your opinion about this thing?" I don't know anything about it; I haven't any opinion. But if somebody comes along who needs light, somebody who wants help for his soul's salvation, and that very thing is a thing that is going to help him out, the Spirit of the Lord will bring it, and it will be as clear as daylight, and you will see it, and all you have to do is just simply to read off to that man, or that congregation, just what you see by the Spirit of the Lord,—what the Spirit brings to your remembrance. But it does not bring that which we have not been giving our minds to; and that throws upon us a responsibility of keeping our minds upon the Word of God, of giving ourselves to the Word of God and to prayer, so that we may be ready for every good work; so that whatever condition a man may be in, whatever need, whatever distress of mind, we will have so studied the Word of God that although we may never have seen that man, we have the Word that meets his case exactly.

Now, we do not have to go around burdened with a sense of how much we know, and with everything parceled, and each one of these things labeled in our minds; this subject is here, and that subject is there. We cannot get at truth in that way. But it is all there as light, and when the Spirit of God shows the occasion and the person, they all meet together; we are ready for every good work. It is not we, but the Spirit of God; and we can put ourselves into the channel and be used by the Spirit of the Lord.

Study Number Sixteen
(Sunday Afternoon, February 28, 1897)

We will pass along in the reading of the book of Hebrews, and find perhaps as we do so, further ground for this statement, "I will put my trust in him." We have already considered the first part of the third chapter. We can briefly cover the remainder. The thought in the first chapter is the faithfulness of Christ, and we by steadfast faith being made a part of his house:—

Wherefore (as the Holy Ghost saith, Today if ye will hear his voice, harden not your hearts as in the provocation, in the day of temptation in the wilderness: when your fathers tempted me, proved me, and saw my works forty years. Wherefore I was grieved with that generation, and said, They do alway err in their hearts; and they have not known my ways. So I sware in my wrath, They shall not enter into my rest.)

You will notice here we have verses seven to eleven in parentheses, so that it reads, "Wherefore take heed brethren, lest there be in any of you an evil heart of unbelief, in departing from the living God." Moses was faithful in the house of God, but the others were unfaithful; they proved the Lord, they tempted him, they tried him, and saw his works for forty years, and yet they did not learn his ways. That was long enough for anybody to learn God's ways. How do we learn the ways of any person?—By seeing what he does.

They saw the Lord's works for forty years, and yet they did not know his ways. That seems wonderful, does it not? Well, I have known people who have seen the ways and works of God for twice forty years, and yet they did not know his ways. It is a very common thing for people to see the works of God and yet not know his ways. The Lord has been showing his works to the people all the time. One of the things that seems so difficult, even right here among us, for the people to believe is that the Lord's ways can be learned by looking at his works. If you cannot know him that way, how can you know him? And yet people will see the works of God before their eyes everywhere day after day, for forty years, and sometimes twice forty years, and never know the Lord's ways. Let us learn the Lord's ways. In his Word he says, My ways are not your ways; and yet we will get together and try to make ourselves believe that our way of doing a thing is the Lord's way. Did you ever think of it? is there not a field of thought in this, that in the Lord's works we are to learn his ways, his ways of working? That is, as we look out and see the works of the Lord everywhere, is there anything in that for us to learn as workers together with him?

The Lord is very quiet in his work. Some of the most mighty works of the Lord are done in the most quiet and unnoticeable way. He does not always rend rocks and make the earth quake when he does a thing. He can do that when he wishes to. And yet the Lord can do just as mighty works without anybody feeling any tremor whatever. Take it in the springtime, when the whole earth is in motion by the coming-up plants. There is a power infinitely beyond measurement and beyond conception, the Lord himself working, and yet all is still and quiet.

What was the result of the children of Israel seeing the works of God and yet not learning his ways? What followed as a consequence?—They did not enter into the rest. "So I sware in my wrath, they shall not enter into my rest." Is the Lord arbitrary in any of his ways?—No. How do his laws originate?—They are his life. Does the Lord sit down and devise laws, and say, "This is what I will impose upon the people? This will be a good thing for them, and I will impose it upon them, and if they don't do it I will cut them off?"—No. The Lord is life, and his life is law. His life is always the same, and it can never be any different from what it is. God's law is as it is, just because he is, and he cannot be other than he is. Whosoever therefore, rejects his life, must as a necessary consequence have death. It cannot be otherwise. It is so because it is so. It is not arbitrary punishment put upon man, but there is nothing else that can be done. If a man will not have life, he must have death.

What is the thing these people would have had, if they had in the works of God learned his ways?—They would have had rest. But since they would not learn his ways as they saw his works, the Lord says, You cannot have rest. They could not enter into his rest. It was an impossibility. "Wherefore take heed brethren, lest there be in any of you an evil heart of unbelief in departing from the living God, but exhort one another daily, while it is called Today." Today is the only time given us. Yesterday does not exist, and there is no such day as tomorrow.

When we come to what we designate tomorrow, it is today. The only time there is in the whole world is today. Whatever the day of the week, it is today always, today.

But exhort one another daily, while it is called Today; lest any of you be hardened through the deceitfulness of sin. For we are made partakers of Christ, if we hold the beginning of our confidence steadfast unto the end; while it is said, Today if ye will hear his voice, harden not your hearts, as in the provocation. For some, when they had heard, did provoke: howbeit not all that came out of Egypt by Moses. But with whom was he grieved forty years? was it not with them that had sinned, whose carcasses fell in the wilderness? And to whom sware he that they should not enter into his rest, but to them that believed not? So we see that they could not enter in because of unbelief.

Not that he would not let them; but they could not. We read on:—

Let us therefore fear, lest, a promise being left us of entering into his rest, any of you should come short of it.

Whose rest had they the opportunity of entering into, and would not?—God's. What was preached to us?—The gospel. What gospel?—The same as unto them. It is no new gospel. There is no room for talk about their having had no chance to hear the gospel. They had it first, and rejected it, and now the gospel is preached unto us as it was unto them; we have just as good a chance as they. When it was preached to them, why did it not profit them? "Not being mixed with faith in them that heard it." It was not joined by faith to them that heard. For who enter into the rest?

(Voices) We who believe.

We; when do we enter into rest?—When we believe. Into whose rest do we enter?—God's rest. The reason why they did not enter in, is because rest comes by faith. They did not believe; therefore they could never rest. But we who believe do enter into rest. What is the proof that believers do enter into God's rest?—The proof here given is, that God swore that the unbelievers should not enter in. That is the negative side of the oath. It is simply the reverse of the oath to Abraham, that he and his seed should enter into rest. In the fifteenth chapter of Genesis we have the promise, and in the twenty-second chapter we have the promise, confirmed by the oath, that the seed of Abraham should have rest from all their enemies. This oath was because of Abraham's faith. So the oath has a double aspect. They who believe enter into rest, and they who do not believe cannot enter into God's rest.

They could not enter into rest, "although the works were finished from the foundation of the world." The statement is that they could not enter into God's rest, although the works were finished from the foundation of the world. Here we find a *seeming* change of subjects from rest to works.

(A voice) I would like to know what is the meaning of that word, "rest."

Rest simply means rest; I do not know of any other meaning for the word. I think we all know by experience something of the meaning of rest, even if it be only by the desire for it.

(A voice) But I am not a preacher.

Well, you do not have to be a preacher in order to believe. We who believe enter into the rest.

(A voice) The question in my mind is, Does it refer to the thousand years' rest?

It is God's rest, and that is not merely for a thousand years, but for eternity.

The works were finished from the foundation of the world. When the works were finished, what followed?—Rest. If a man has a work to do, and he finishes it, what must necessarily follow?—Rest. He can do nothing else. Man does not finish his work. Therefore, he finds no rest in his own work.

Elder Frederickson.—Is this the same rest as where it says, "Come unto me, all ye that labor and are heavy laden, and I will give you rest"?

Whose rest are we talking about?—The Lord's. Who says, Come unto me, and I will give you rest?—The Lord. Then it must be the same rest. When you come to one of these fundamental principles, believe it. Make it your own by faith, and cling to it, and believe it forever; then you can go through the Bible, and faith will lighten it up, all the time. We cannot fight or argue our way into an understanding of the Word of God; but just as the sun melts the ice, so we believe our way into an understanding of the Bible.

God calls us to rest on the assurance that the rest is prepared, because the work is finished. When work is all done, and well done, then rest must follow, because there is nothing else to do. If there is more to do, then the work is not finished.

We are taken back to the first chapter of Genesis, to see whether or not we believe what we cry out so much against the evolutionists for not believing—the simple story of creation. The first step in the proof that the rest is ready is that the works are finished. What is the evidence of it?—For he spake in a certain place of the seventh day on this wise: And God did rest on the seventh day from all his works. And in this place again, they shall not enter into my rest. Who is it that speaks?—God. What is he talking about?—His rest. When did he rest?—When his works were finished. On what day did he rest?—The seventh day. The seventh day is the Sabbath of the Lord thy God. Sabbath means rest, so the Sabbath-day is the Lord's rest.

Take the fourth and fifth verses together:—

For he spake in a certain place of the seventh day on this wise, And God did rest the seventh day from all his works. And in this place again, If they shall enter into my rest.

They cannot rest. They cannot keep the Sabbath day. Is not that what is said? They cannot rest because of unbelief. We which believe do enter into rest, because the works were finished, and therefore the works prepared, from the foundation of the world. God rested the seventh day from *all* his works. That is what he said of the seventh day in one place; in another place he said of it, "They shall not enter into his rest."

Closing up the record of the work which God did during creation week in the first chapter of Genesis,—

God saw everything that he had made, and, behold, it was very good.

God was pleased with it. He did not see where he could make it any better. It was perfect. Whatsoever God does is done forever. Nothing can be added to it, nothing taken from it.

Now we are going to get rest. We are going to get the rest of the Lord. But the rest must necessarily be preceded by works—works of what character, what kind?—Works that are perfect, finished and complete. Take the scripture that we have here, "We which believe do enter into rest," and compare it with what the Saviour said in the sixth chapter of John, in answer to the Pharisees' question, "What shall we do, that we might work the works of God?" Did he say, If you want to work the works of God, do some works? Did he say, If you will believe, you can do the works of God?—Oh, no. He said, "This is the work of God, that ye believe on him whom he hath sent." God has never told anybody to do his works, because God knows enough to know that nobody else can do his work. It is only men who put themselves in the place of God that say, "We can do anything that the Lord can do; we can do work, and do it just as good as God can do it; we can be justified by works; we can do works that will stand by the side of God's work, and he can't tell the difference." God knows enough to know that there is no other being in the universe that can do his works, and he does not ask us to do them. But "this is the work of God; that ye believe in him whom he hath sent." Now, is there any contradiction in these texts, namely, "This is the work of God, that ye believe;" and "We which believe do enter into rest?"—No. Why?—Because the work is done; and when you get the work of God, you get the work that is finished, and therefore you have rest. Therefore by believing we get rest in the perfect, the finished, work of God.

Let us notice the text referred to a moment ago:—

Come unto me, all ye that labor and are heavy laden, and I will give you rest. Take my yoke upon you, and learn of me, for I am meek and lowly in heart, and ye shall find rest.

Find rest in meekness and lowliness, for my yoke is easy, and my burden is light. Therefore that which worries us, and tires us, is this pride of life that makes us think that we can and must do everything ourselves. But we can't do it, and that is why it tires us. Suppose we have a piece of work given us to do, and we have labored at it faithfully, and then when we have finished it, we find a botched job. Can you ever get any satisfaction out of it? Do you ever get any rest from it?—No; you do not rest over it, because you are held to do that work, and you can't rest at night because you think, Now I have to do that work over again. And when you do it over again, even then it is not good.

Who is there that wholly finishes and completes all his daily round of work. Who is it that finishes it perfectly, so that he can look back upon it in perfect satisfaction, and take absolute rest and enjoyment in looking at it. Is there anybody?—No. We can't get it done. The best work we can do, there is something that is wrong about it, something that is a failure, something that is incomplete; and that is what tires us. Don't you know that it is a simple fact that it is not the work that men do, so much as the work that they cannot do, that tires them? It is the work they try to do and fail to accomplish that tires them. Not only do we not get our work all done, but we don't do it perfectly even as far as we go, and that is what tires us out. You know there are thousands and thousands of men that say, just ordinary work given to men, ordinary men's work, I can't finish it; do the best I can, I can't finish it. But when they talk about God's work, O, they can do that well enough. Is not there something unreasonable about that? They acknowledge that they cannot do their own work as it ought to be done, but they feel fully competent to do God's work. But what are God's works?—His work is what he does, and everything that he does is right, and therefore righteousness. It is very common for people to think that they can do right; but righteousness is God's work, and the man who can't do his own work, must not suppose that he can do God's work.

We are heavy laden with sin, and that which wearies us is our vain attempt to work out righteousness. So long as we keep at that work, our work must be incomplete; and so of course we don't find rest. Who is there that has not said, "Now, if I had that to do over again…?" and then follows a list of improvements that he would make. A man makes a machine, and it is no sooner done than he begins to see where he can improve on it the next time. But the first time that God did his work, it was just as good as it was possible to be done. He could not see anything incomplete about it. It was all right. He did not wish that he could do it over again. It was all done, and well done; therefore the only thing that could follow was rest. How had God done his work in the first place?—By his Word. "He spake, and it was." And he could rest in confidence in his own Word. He had confidence that the Word which created could uphold, so he rested, and took satisfaction in looking at the work he had done.

The Lord made man also just as good as he knew how to make him, and we read in Gen.2:15,—

And the Lord took the man, and put him into the garden of Eden to dress it and to keep it.

If we had a strictly literal rendering of that, it would be, "He caused him to rest in the garden of Eden, to dress it and to keep." God gave man work to do in Eden, so that work is no part of the curse. It was work upon the land, too. That is the only kind of work God gave to man. He put him in the garden of Eden to work, but he caused him to rest there. The whole world was given man, but the garden of Eden was the place which was his home. He caused him to rest there, to dress it, and to keep it. Now mark, he didn't have to make the garden. God made it, and man had only to keep. When we see how he came to lose it, we can see how he was to keep it. His sin was unbelief. He didn't believe God, therefore he lost the perfect work of God. How, then, could he have kept it? Just by belief. "This is the work of God, that ye believe." So long as he believed, so long he would keep the garden and have it for his own: so long would he have the perfect work of God, so long he would have rest in that garden. No matter how much he worked, if he worked from morning till night, he never got tired. That is the beauty of God's work. Because the work was all finished, it was all perfect and complete, therefore in keeping that work he did not get tired. Here was a work finished and given to him, and all he had to do was to rest in it and keep it as it was. His very work was rest.

Now, in the second chapter of Ephesians we have a word about salvation.

> For by grace are ye saved through faith, and that not of yourselves. It is the gift of God. Not of works, lest any man should boast.

Not of whose works?—Not our works. Why?—"Lest any man should boast." But it is of works, nevertheless. "For we are his workmanship." So it is works after all. *But* whose works?—God's works. But there is no chance for God to boast over God. "For we are his workmanship, created in Christ Jesus unto good works, which God hath before ordained that we should walk in them." That was the case with Adam when God made him. He was created in Christ Jesus for good works. Who made them?—God. And he made them for the purpose that he might walk in them and enjoy them. Now, the gospel is to bring us back, is that we may have that rest in the finished and perfect works of God.

When God had his work all finished and complete, what did he do?—He rested from all his works. But that rest, that work, was the new earth. God's rest, then, pertains to the new earth. The Sabbath on which God rested was the Sabbath of the new earth, of Eden,—Eden rest.

We will take all the verses in Hebrews 4 in order presently, but we have not time today. So we pass to the ninth verse. Just that simple statement, "There remaineth a rest." Many read it as though it said there will come a rest to the people of God. But what does the word "remain" mean?—Something that is left; something that still exists from a previous time. When the rest was given to man, the whole earth was new. There was no curse upon it. Now sin has come, and the earth has become old, and is cursed; but nevertheless there remains a rest to the people of God. That rest comes from Eden. Eden has never had any curse upon it. Man's sin brought curse upon the earth, but drove him out of Eden. There is one spot pertaining to the earth which was never touched by the curse. Eden is now in heaven, the paradise of God, where God's throne is; and Christ himself is there, the man Christ Jesus, who was made lower than the angels for the suffering of death, crowned as man with glory and honor, and set over the works of God's hand in Eden: and he is the one who says, "Come unto me, all ye that labor and are heavy laden, and I will give you rest."

The rest in Eden was Sabbath rest. The Sabbath is a bit of Eden that remains to us until Eden is restored again; and he who keeps the Sabbath as God keeps it, as God gave it to be kept, has the rest that the Lord Jesus Christ has in heaven.

But how can one keep it?—By faith. Because rest means work finished, and the work is God's work. God himself finished it. Then we could not do it if we should try. So there are two reasons why we could not do the work: in the first place, only God can do God's work; and in the second place, it is already done, so when you get there you do not find anything to do. It is done already. Now when God rested from it, what presumption for man to try to do it! Therefore the thing being finished, we get it by faith. Now he says to some, You cannot enter into my rest, because they do not believe and cease from their own works by taking his.

(Voices) How, then, are we to be workers together with God?

By resting in him.

(Another voice) That verse referred to in Matthew says, Come unto me all ye that labor, and I will give you rest; and the next verse says, Take my yoke upon you. Does that mean work?

Yes; certainly. But he says, "My yoke is easy, and my burden is light." What is his burden?—He carries the whole world. But he carries it easily. Now he says, Learn of Me. If you carry the burden, what does it do?—It galls your shoulders, and makes you tired and irritable and fretful. He says, Do not do that way. Learn of me. He works, but it does not worry him. Now who is going to complain about work if it does not worry him—work that you can do and not get tired doing? Who is going to complain about it? It is a pleasure to do that. There is solid enjoyment in it. There is large satisfaction, and that is what the Lord wants us to have.

We have been talking about the message for a long time, and when we speak of the third angel's message, then everybody thinks about the Sabbath. But a little while ago we read that justification by faith was the message, and many people have thought that if we preached justification by faith, we could say nothing about the Lord's coming or the Sabbath. Why, brethren, we want to learn the message. Let us see how many here have heard people say when you preach the Sabbath, "Yes, but you know that we are not justified by works." Have you not all heard that?

(Voices) Yes.

And they thought that proved that we should not keep the Sabbath, not realizing that there is a great difference between rest and works. The Sabbath is rest, not a work. Sabbath-keeping is not justification by works, but justification by rest—by rest in the finished work of God in Christ. The Sabbath is rest. It is God's rest. It is perfect rest. It is rest that justifies because it is rest that brings perfect works, God's works. Our works are good for nothing. We cannot do anything. "Not of works, lest any man should boast." "We are his workmanship."

Somebody says, "Well, I don't believe it is necessary for me to keep the Sabbath. The Lord says to such an one, You cannot keep it, for only those who believe enter into rest. Mark this, brethren, the Sabbath is such a glorious thing that when people see it, they delight in it; and we do the Lord an injustice, and the people an injustice, when we present it in such a way that they think that it is a burden, a task. It is not something the Lord has imposed upon people, but a benefit that he has conferred on them. What man is there in all this world that complains because he is obliged to rest?

Then, instead of its being a hard thing, especially for the laboring class, to keep the Sabbath, it is a blessing for them. It is the laboring man's friend. It is rest. It is the thing that will bring him out of all his difficulties quicker than any political party or any labor party ever dreamed of helping him out of them. And this is the reason why Seventh-day Adventists of all people in the world, have absolutely nothing to do with any political party in existence. Their platforms are quack remedies, and God does not want us to deal in them. He wants us to deal in that which is true. Political parties claim to be the friend of the working men; they claim that they will make better times, that they will make it easier for the people. That is what they are all working for. Now the Lord comes in with his gospel, which promises us all rest; which promises every man his own garden spot, and not only his own garden spot, but every man the inheritance of the whole earth, and all men an inheritance in the whole world in such a way that there will be no question about property rights, but every man will have free inheritance and absolute rest, a wealth without limit.

Rest, rest in labor, better than any labor party ever thought possible; for the best thing we can think of is to shorten the hours of labor, so that man can have more time for rest. But God promises to give a man rest all the time he is working. That is better. And this we can be absolutely sure will be brought about in a much shorter time than any politician ever dreamed that his schemes could be brought to completion. Who is there that, knowing such a thing, will be such a fool as to spend his time over that which promises him nothing. Why should we waste our time on something which at the best is nothing but a quack remedy, when we have something that will solve every difficulty under heaven?

Now mark, Sabbath-keeping is rest, God's rest, because his work is finished, completed. What kind of works are God's works?—Perfect works. And how do we get these works?—By faith. So Sabbath-keeping means faith. It means righteousness by faith. Then that is the message. Righteousness by faith is the message. There are lots of people who believe in righteousness by faith in Christ, but who do not see anything about the Sabbath. Now what we have to show them is that Sabbath-keeping means the perfection of God's work, and therefore the perfection of rest in him by faith.

Now take the finished work. What does the cross of Christ do for men?—"If any man be in Christ, he is a new creature." So in the cross of Christ we see a new creation. That is what the cross does. The preaching of Christ is to them that perish, foolishness, but to those who are saved it is the power of God. Where do we see the power of God manifested.—In the creation, in the things he has made. So the power of Christ is the power of creation, creative power. Now the perfect work of God, this new creation, was lost by sin. Sabbath-keeping commemorates God's works, not as we see them now, but God's perfect work. But the curse came and destroyed them. "Christ hath redeemed us from the curse, being made a curse for us" in the suffering of death. On the cross Christ redeems us from the curse by bringing to us the works without the curse, the perfect work of God. Therefore when Christ was nailed upon the cross, what were the last words he uttered?—"It is finished." What?—The new creation. It is all complete. So coming to the cross we have the perfection of God's new creation in Christ. But the Sabbath is a commemoration of the new creation. Therefore the Sabbath is the sign of the perfect rest, nay, it is the very rest itself, which God gives us in Christ.

Just one more text that we can read today before we close. In the fifty-eighth chapter of Isaiah:—

If thou turn away thy foot from the Sabbath, from doing thy pleasure on my holy day, and call the Sabbath a delight, the holy of the Lord, honorable; and shalt honor him, not doing thine own ways, nor finding thine own pleasure, nor speaking thine own words: then shalt thou delight thyself in the Lord.

What does Eden mean?—Delight, pleasure. The Sabbath comes from Eden, and is a part of Eden, and therefore it is a delight. In it we get the very same delightful rest that God had in the beginning in looking at his own perfect work.

We have only begun to study the Sabbath today. Tomorrow, if the Lord will, we shall see further into the details of what Sabbath-keeping means, what it is, and then we can understand better what our work as Seventh-day Adventists, what the work of the Lord is, what the message is. But I think anybody here can see that the third angel's message is righteousness by faith; for the Sabbath is righteousness by faith; for by it a man comes into God's works, and those works are perfect. Therefore he gets rest by faith. But the man who does not believe the Lord, cannot get rest. Is it then possible for a man to keep the Sabbath and not believe the Lord implicitly?—No, sir. He stops work on the last day of the week, and that is all that can be said of him. If he does not believe God, then he cannot keep the Sabbath.

Now just one thing more to show this clearly. He who does not believe the Lord, what does he say about God?—He has made him a liar. Of course, not absolutely, actually, a liar, for God cannot lie. But the man who says that God is a liar, is himself a liar. Now, will the man who is a liar make a very good Sabbath-keeper? There is no other way to keep the Sabbath, except to believe the Lord.

Study Number Seventeen
(Monday Afternoon, March 1, 1897)

What is left to us?—A rest, or a promise of entering into rest. Whose rest?—God's rest. Who has entered into rest?—They who believe. When do they enter into rest?—When they cease from their own works. And when does one cease from his own works?—When be believes. "For we which believe do enter into rest." What is the evidence that the rest is ready?—Because the works were finished from the foundation of the world. What is the evidence that the works were then finished?—Because God rested on the seventh day from all his works. And that this is the rest which God gives his people is shown from the fact that, still speaking of the seventh day, he says of unbelievers, They shall not enter into my rest.

For he spake in a certain place of the seventh day on this wise, And God did rest the seventh day from all his works. And in this place again, If they shall enter into my rest.

What is he talking about in both places?—The seventh day. In one place he says of the seventh day, that God rested on the seventh day from all his works; and in another place he says of it, "They shall not enter into my rest." When did God rest on the seventh day?—When he finished his work at the close of the six days of creation. What was the state of his works then?—They were very good. The earth was new, so that the rest of God pertains to the new earth, the new earth state. To be more exact, we should say that the new creation is the rest.

Now what did Christ say about the works of God?—"This is the work of God that ye believe." But what is the characteristic of all of God's works?—They are perfect. They are just as good as they can be. Moreover, God rested from all his works, so that they are complete—nothing can be added to them, and nothing can be taken away from them; and when we truly believe, we get those works; but since God's works are finished works, and so perfect that there can be no amendment, therefore he who gets the works of God, gets the rest of God. One of the perfect works which God made in the beginning, was man himself Man was God's workmanship, created in Christ, Jesus unto good works; and those good works were created in Christ. God had already completed them, even before man was made. The works were finished from the foundation of the world, and man could walk in them, and walking in them, they would continually have rest in the rest of the Lord.

But man fell, the works were lost, and the curse came upon all. Christ redeems us from the curse, being made a curse for us, and he was made a curse for us in being hung upon a tree. And so in him, in his cross, the new creation is effected,] we become new creatures. In the cross, then, we find the finished works of God, perfect and complete, that which man lost by sin. In the cross of Christ there is perfect rest, because in it the works are finished. Christ said, "It is finished." Every one comes to Christ, finds there the perfect work, and finding that perfect work of God finished and complete, he gets rest.

As we said, the rest of God is the new creation. Now mark: What works are they which we get in Christ?—God's finished works, the new creation. The very same works, then, that were finished from the foundation of the world. Therefore, in the cross in Christ, we are brought to the very same rest. The cross of Christ brings us right back to the creation, drops out, swallows up, and obliterates all the infinite blackness, and sin, and curse, and brings us right back again—to the new creation, to the same works, and therefore to the same rest as at the beginning. When the cross of Christ is preached, when the gospel is preached, there is no room whatever for anybody to say that the Sabbath was abolished at the cross? How could anybody imagine such a thing? The objection is taken away before it has a chance to be made, because in the cross of Christ we are brought to the rest which was ready from the foundation of the world, because the works were finished then. So the fourth chapter of Hebrews is the strongest Sabbath chapter in the Bible. But there is just as much in it for us to learn as there is for anybody else, because we who talk about the Sabbath must learn what the Sabbath is. It is God's rest, and his rest has not taint of the curse in it. It has no imperfection in it; it is perfection itself.

We are God's workmanship, created in Christ Jesus unto good works, God's good works, and these good works were prepared from the beginning, that we should walk in them. Walking in those good works already prepared and finished, we shall be having continual rest, the rest of the Lord. The Sabbath from the beginning, — and it is always the same as it was in the beginning, we must always go back there for the correct condition of everything, — the Sabbath is to mark God's finished work. It, then, is God's righteousness which man gets as a gift.

We see, then, that the man who does not believe the Lord, does not keep the Sabbath. He cannot keep the Sabbath; it is simply impossible. The Sabbath marks God's finished, new creation; therefore the Sabbath is the seal of perfection. The keeping of the Sabbath, then, is simply the partaking of God's perfection. See here: there is no opportunity for any one to say, "Well, you keep the Sabbath, expecting to be saved by it?—No, not by any means; because the Sabbath itself is evidence of the fact that God is Creator,—that he creates all things in Christ, and that man has no power. The keeping of the Sabbath is the acknowledgment of the fact that we can't do anything. All we can do is to take what God has done for us. We have the statement, "Remember the Sabbath day [remember the day of the Sabbath] to keep it holy." This commandment instead of being a burden to the poor laboring man, is a blessing to him above all others.

The poor man who has nothing on earth in which to trust, who from day to day has nothing but his day's work between him and ruin,—to him the Sabbath comes bringing the knowledge of God as the Creator and Preserver. He rests upon the seventh day not as a task, as a burden which God has laid upon him, but as a benefit which God has conferred upon him, because he knows the Lord so well, has so seen the Lord in his perfection, that he can trust him perfectly, knowing that he cannot do anything for himself, and that he is not obliged to depend on himself. Not even if he gained all his daily bread, is he able to do anything; but it comes from God? God provides it for him, and he simply gathers what God gives him; that is the lesson God desires us to learn. Of the birds and beasts the Psalmist says, "That thou givest them, they gather: thou openest thine hand, they are filled with good." The bird earns its living, just as much as man does. Yet how many men wish that they did not have any more care than the birds. They have just as much care as man need have. He has to work all day to provide for himself and those who depend upon him; but you say all the birds have to do is to pick their food. Yes; but that is all that a man has to do. He works and gathers, and then prides himself upon his superiority over birds; whereas the bird is the better off of the two, because the bird does not trust to himself, but trusts in the Lord. A man has to depend upon the Lord, but does not give the credit to him.

(A voice) What was that text referred to?

Psalms 104:28. It refers not only to birds, but to all the beasts. "That thou givest them they gather: thou openest thine hand, they are filled with good." So the Lord opens his hands, and people come and take, that is all. The man does not make it, or create it. God speaks to the earth, it brings forth abundantly, and man picks it up, that is all.

Now as to the keeping of the Sabbath: The Sabbath comes to this poor man, to make God known to him. "I gave them my Sabbaths, to be a sign between me and them, that they might know that I am the Lord that sanctify them." Eze. 20:12. It shows us God's power to sanctify us, by showing that to him we owe our existence and its continuance. We leave out one day's work entirely, to show what?—That we depend upon the Lord; that we take his Word, believe it, live upon it, and then, although to human calculation it may seem impossible for us to live if we keep Sabbath; may seem to be the ruin of us, because we shall probably lose our work, and have no prospect of getting anything more, the poor man can simply say, I live by the Word of the Lord, I trust him, he is the one who gives me my daily bread; therefore I will trust him for everything, and, as an indication of that fact, I will rest right here, according to his Word. Do you see? The Sabbath stands for perfect trust in the Lord. Remember the Sabbath day to keep it holy,—to how many days in the week does that apply? —; Every day. The Sabbath is the seventh day, but the keeping of the Sabbath has reference to every day of the week; because, if I rest my body on the seventh day, and on the second or third or fourth day of the week I doubt the Lord, what does that mean?—Unrest. God himself has worked for me, for man's support not only for a little while, but for eternity. When we mistrust the Lord, we forget that fact. Is a man trusting in the Lord when he is fretting or worrying, for fear this or that thing will not come out right?—No. Then when a man begins to worry and to go with a long face, what is he doing?—Breaking the Sabbath. He is not remembering the Sabbath, to keep it holy. He has the burden upon himself. Christ says, Come, and learn of me. My burden is light. What is his burden?—He bears the sins of the world, yea, the world itself. But he says, My burden is light. All the work and worry, the turmoil and sin, everything in the world, he bears it all and bears it easily.

Now, we have very little of the world upon us, but it is awfully heavy, isn't it? Men sometimes think they have the whole world upon their shoulders, and that they have got to bear it. I do not know of any people on earth that are more liable to think they are overburdened, than Seventh-day Adventist preachers; why, you meet a conference president sometimes, and you would think that he had just come from a funeral. They have a burden bearing upon them, wearing them out. They have a burden in the work of the Lord; but what does Christ say?—Learn of me. He did not worry. He had as much on his shoulders, on his mind, as any ordinary person; he had as many persons coming to him and taking his time, but he did not worry, did not get excited, or agitated and flurried; no, not a bit of it; and he says, "Come, and learn of me. My burden is light." It did not worry him at all. He could carry it so easily. That is keeping the Sabbath, resting in the Lord, depending upon him. Why?—Because he has done the work. We yoke up with him, and work with him, so that he does the works in us, and that makes the work easy, the burden light.

We will now pass along rapidly in the chapter: —

"Seeing therefore it remaineth that some must enter therein,"—into what?—The rest of God. But that rest is what?—Sabbath rest. But the Sabbath rest which comes to us (ninth verse),—"there remaineth therefore a rest,"—of what is that a part?—A part of the new earth. That is all. A part of the new creation, a bridge from the time that paradise was lost until paradise is restored. Every one that will keep the Sabbath is lifted up out of this pit into which we have fallen, to the light and joy and glory and blessing of the new earth, to taste the power of the world to come. Here we have the same thing as in the second chapter. "Unto the angels hath he not put into subjection the world to come;" but he has put it in subjection to the man Christ Jesus, and to us in him. In him we find Sabbath-keeping, because in him is found the new earth rest. Now it remains that some *must* enter in. In am glad of that. Not "some *may*;" "some *must*." God has pledged himself. God is under obligations, not to man, but to himself; because he swore by himself. Some must come and enter that rest, in order to save his word in order to save God from breaking his oath. It must be so.

Now, that gives me courage. Some *must* enter in, the necessity that some must enter into rest is so great that the invitation is, Whosoever will, let him come; take anybody; the urgency is so great, that anybody in the world who will come can come and find rest. No matter what his condition, or what he has done, God says, Let him come, and I will take him. It is not an exclusive thing. It is not, Somebody may come in; there is room for a few, and we will take a selected few; but some *must* enter. There *must* be some recruits, therefore come along, everybody who will; come in and find rest. It must be that some enter in, and they to whom it was first preached entered not in because of unbelief, therefore the promise is left to us. For we know that had they believed, the work would have been finished hundreds of years ago, and the earth would have been restored. But because they did not enter in —

Again, he limiteth a certain day, saying in David, Today after so long a time; as it is said, Today if we will hear his voice, harden not your hearts.

Why is there another day limited?

What is the object of that other day?—To give man another opportunity to accept God's rest; for some must enter in, and he will give them another day in which to come. It is the day of salvation. and the only day of salvation is *Today*. "This is the day which the Lord hath made; we will rejoice and be glad in it." Open the gates of righteousness, and we will enter in. This day is for us to enter into God's righteousness. Praise the Lord Let us be glad and rejoice in it.

For if, Jesus (Joshua) had given them rest, then would he not afterward have spoken of another day.

There would have been no need of it,if Joshua had given them rest, and they had believed; that would have ended the matter. Jesus and Joshua are one word both meaning deliverer, saviour. It was not an accident that the one chosen to lead the people into the land of Canaan was named Joshua. Now here we have Joshua (Jesus) who does give us rest. In him we find perfect rest, even the rest of the world to come. By the way we love what the Lord has for us *now* by looking too for ahead. Now I do not want to start anybody to criticizing people's prayers; but I often think that the forms of expression that people fall into indicate perhaps something of their state of mind and in turn react upon their thinking. I do not know how extensive it is among people generally, but I think among us—and we are the last people in the world who should use it—you will find perhaps nine-tenths of the prayers close with, "Save us at last." Now it does not worry me a particle about being saved at last, because if the Lord saves me now, from day to day, it will be all right in the end. If the Lord saves us at the present time, we need have no fear about the last. But I sometimes fear that we have our eyes fixed so for ahead, and desire so much to be saved at last, that we forget all about being saved now. Some say, "If I can only be saved at last in the kingdom of God, I shall be satisfied." If I am saved now, I am satisfied. We put off the time of satisfaction. We are content to be dissatisfied now, if we can be satisfied hereafter. But I would rather be satisfied all the time.

So the Lord gives us heavenly rest in which to gain heaven. He gives us heaven here on this earth. "There remaineth therefore a rest to the people of God. For he that is entered into his rest, he also hath ceased from his own works, as God did from his." Now, when he has ceased from his own works, what works does he have? who works him?—Why, God's works, and God's works will be manifested in him. That which makes us weary, and always weak in what we call the Lord's work, is trying to perfect our own works. That is a thing that cannot be done, and the man who tries it worries himself out of it; but when he lets go, and lets God work in him, he can rest all the time in confidence in God.

"Let us therefore give diligence to enter into his rest, lest any man fall after the same example of unbelief," for unbelief keeps us from the work, and so from the rest of the Lord. "Is that rest present or future?"—That depends on us. If we have not entered into rest, of course rest is in the future for us, How far in the future is it?—Just as far in the future as our unbelief continues. If our unbelief continues forever, it will never come. If our unbelief ceases now, then the rest is for us now.

(A voice) What kind of labor must we do to enter into that rest?

Of course that is only a technical question because the literal rendering of the word is, Let us give diligence, instead of "Let us labor." But yet we may take it as it is, and the question is easily answered. "This is the work of God, that ye believe." That is the kind of work we are to do to enter into rest, because we who have believed, do enter into that rest. We get the rest by works, it is true, because rest must be preceded by works. What kind of works precede the rest?—Complete works; because if the work is not done, then you cannot rest. A man cannot rest from his work before it is done. He may stop because he is obliged to stop for a while, but he cannot rest from the work before the work is finished. Then if we are going to have perfect rest, it must be from a work that is finished. But whose work only is finished and perfect?—God's work. We cannot do anything as it ought to be done. Therefore we may as well stop first as last, and accept God's work, because that is the work that gives us rest.

Study Number Eighteen
(Tuesday Afternoon, March 2, 1897)

Let us labor therefore to enter into that rest, lest any man fall after the same example of unbelief. For the word of God is quick, and powerful, and sharper than any two-edged sword, piercing even to the dividing asunder of soul and spirit, and of the joints and marrow, and is a discerner of the thoughts and intents of the heart. Neither is there any creature that is not manifest in his sight: but all things are naked and opened unto the eyes of him with whom we have to do. Seeing then that we have a great high priest, that is passed into the heavens, Jesus the Son of God, let us hold fast our profession. For we have not an high priest which cannot be touched with the feeling of our infirmities; but was in all points tempted like as we are, yet without sin. Let us therefore come boldly unto the throne of grace, that we may obtain mercy, and find grace to help in time of need.

We need to have the whole of this in our minds at one time. Rest has been laid out before us, God's own rest; think of it. God calls us to enjoy his own rest, just as he gives us his own peace. Let us give diligence therefore to enter into rest. Now somebody with that verse before him, and with his finger on it, will ask, How are we going to do that? how are we going to labor? whose labor is it? how are we going to labor, by which we enter into rest? There is no chance for any question if you look at it; think what it says: "Lest any man fall after the same example of unbelief,???????". For we which believe do enter into rest. How do we labor to enter into rest?—Believe. This is the work of God, that ye believe. Faith is the labor that brings rest. Faith comes by hearing, and hearing by the Word of God. So what is it upon which we rest, and which gives the rest?—The Word of God. For the word of God is living, powerful, active. Instead of "active," suppose we take the original Greek word, simply transferred, and not translated. The original word is "energy." The Word of God is energetic, or, it is energy; that is better. The Word of God is living, and it is energy. This thought is conveyed to us in the connection: Let us give diligence to enter into rest, lest we fall after the example of unbelief, for the Word of God is living, it is energy. Now, what lesson is there in that?—Let the Word work, because there is energy in it. So when we read the Word of God, let us receive it as it is indeed, the Word of God which effectually worketh in them who believe.

The farthest away from this truth is when we think we must do the work ourselves, leaving the Word of God out of the question. The next step is supposed to be a wonderful advance; namely, when people think they can take the word and world it themselves. But the word itself works, and our rest is in letting it work in us.

You know that Word in Col. 3:16; "Let the word of Christ dwell in you richly in all wisdom." It seems to me that that would be a thing that we would jump at, such a prospect as that, expressing, as we so often do, our sense of lack of knowledge. We say that we cannot see, that we do not know what to do; and if we really believe that, it seems to me we would eagerly seize this, let the word of Christ dwell in you richly in all wisdom. That is though, all wisdom for us if we will let the word dwell in us. Brethren, it seems to some a wonderfully hard saying for one to say, "You do not believe the Word;" but we do not half believe it, because we read the plain statement of what the Word is, how it furnishes all might and all wisdom, that it is self-existing, living, full of energy, works effectively in the one who receives it and lets it be in him; and yet we do not let it work in us, while professing to desire what it offers. Somebody will say, I cannot see how it is going to work out. Of course you cannot see, and you never will see, and you don't need to see. Let the Word of God dwell in you richly and it will do the work. It is the Word which is to be put into us, implanted in us. The word is a seed for we read, "being born again, not of corruptible seed, but of incorruptible, by the Word of God, which liveth and abideth forever." But we cannot see how it is going to be done, and therefore we do not believe it. When we meet an infidel, and he will say that he does not believe anything but what he can see, we scout the idea, and yet we do the same thing over and over again. If we can't see it, of course it can't be done. Did you ever read in the fourth chapter of Mark, twenty-sixth verse and onward, what the Lord says about the kingdom of God?

"And he said, So is the kingdom of God, as if a man should cast seed into the ground; and should sleep, and rise night and day."

Perfectly content, because he knows exactly how the seed germinates, springs up and bears fruit?—No, it does not say so at all. "And the seed should spring and grow up, he knoweth not how." Isn't it wonderful that farmers can sleep nights? They cast the seed into the ground, and they may say, "I can't see how it's going to grow." Of course they can't, because it is in the ground, and they have no business to see it. It is not for them to see at all. You don't knew how it is going to be done, and you do not need to know how it is going to be done, because you do not have to do it. God is going to do the work, and isn't it enough if he knows how? Suppose somebody gives Brother Kilgore a piece of work to do, and I sit down and groan and they because I do not know how to do that work. He has to do the work, and I fret because I don't know how. Now, we profess to believe that God does the work, but we hold ourselves aloof, because we can't see how he does the work. What business is it of ours, so long as he does it? He has the work to do, and he has the power to do it.

Again: Christ said, "The kingdom of God cometh not with observation: neither shall they say, Lo here! or, lo there? for behold, the kingdom of God is within you." That is it, the two texts fit together perfectly. The seed is the Word of God, and if put into an individual, if he will let it be there,—if he will not insists upon digging it up,—if it is put there and allowed to remain, it grows, and he does not know how. It is not with observation. He can't see it. It is an implanted seed, and he is content to let it grow because he has confidence in the germ of life in that seed that it is energetic and will work its way out. There is a mighty power in a peach seed. Put it into the ground, and that seemingly dead kernel will spring up and grow, we do not know how. But God knows how. You know what the Lord says about the man that can't see, and that is bothering about a thing that is not given him to see. It is the very same question, too, that we have under consideration. Somebody will say "How do the dead rise, and with what body to they come? I don't understand about that. I can't see how it is done." "Thou fool," he says "bothering about what you do not know anything about." For you do not have to raise the deal. God gives it a body. "That which thou sowest is not quickened except it die." "God giveth in a body as it hath pleased him, and to every seed has own body." So when the seed—the Word—is planted in a person, and he lets it be, simply less it dwell in his flesh, God will give this seed a body. "To every seed its own body." It will transform the man in accordance with itself.

The Word of God is living, energetic, sharper than any two-edged sword; because the sharpest two-edged sword can no more than get in between the joints; but the word of God pierces to the dividing asunder of soul and spirit, into ever fiber of the being. There is not a part of the being, there is not an atom so small, but that the Word of God pierces it. Do you believe it? The Word of God is life. It is God's own life, because the Word is God. You see that we come back to our first lessons, the one lesson that we need, because it contains everything. It is the lesson of God in his works, of his word in his works, for the Word is God. The Word of God is not simply certain printed letters. The Word is living. What we have written here is only a form of the Word—a description of the Word, if you please, an accurate description or picture of it; it tells us what the word is, what it will do and what we may expect of it; but the Word itself is life. It is full of motion and energy, and is sharper than any two-edged sword, because it pierces to the dividing asunder of soul and spirit, joints and marrow, and discerns even the thoughts and intents of the heart. There is nothing that is not manifest in his sight, because all things are naked and open to the eyes of him with whom we have to do. Wherever the living power of God is, there is God, with perception, with energy, with sensitiveness. (You understand what I mean by that word "sensitiveness." Not that kind of sensitiveness that men have, that gets hurt every time a person looks at them crosswise, but it is full of feeling and perception.) There is not an atom in the living body but there is the Word of God present because that is the life of the body.

How does God know all about us?—He is there on the spot. "We have not an high priest which cannot be reached with the feeling of our infirmities." Or rather, which cannot have sympathy. That is the Greek word. The word "sympathy" is simply the Greek word transferred, and that is the word which is here used. What does sympathy mean?—It means suffering with. So we have not an high priest which cannot suffer with our infirmities. Leave out the negatives and what do you have?—We *have* an high priest who can suffer, and who does suffer with our infirmities. The Word of God is present in every place, and is bearing the infirmities of the flesh, because the Word of God was made flesh, and feels and knows all that the flesh bears. Wherever there is life, there is God.

Talk about hiding from the Lord. Don't you see it is an impossibility to hide ourselves from God? "Whither shall I flee from thy presence?" It cannot be done, because wherever you go, "thou art there." He knows because he feels. Is there anything that God knows by study and research? Does God, by setting himself to investigate a matter, learn something that he never knew before?—O no; that cannot be, because that would argue imperfection on the part of God. It cannot be. He knows it simply because he knows it; because he exists. He knows how we feel because he feels it. That is the only way anybody can know how another feels. You know this. Nobody can sympathize with another in any affliction unless he has passed through that same affliction. That is plain. Only he who has passed through anything can sympathize and suffer with one. Now, Christ suffers with us in our infirmities. The Word knows us, because it is in us. Every weakness of the human body, every infirmity, everything that touches and affects us, everything that causes us pain, whether it is material or physical, every injury, every wound, everything that depresses us, the Lord knows it and feels it, because he is there. If it were not for God's presence in us, we could not feel anything, because we should have no life. Christ is our life, so that if there is any difference, he feels our pains even more acutely than we do.

Is there anything to rejoice over in that thought? Is there any comfort in that? Why, it is all the comfort in the world. Now put with this Isa 53 : 11, and we shall get one grand, comforting thought: "He shall see of the travail of his soul, and shall be satisfied: by his knowledge shall my righteous servant justify many; for he shall bear their iniquities."

See? By his knowledge you shall justify many, for you shall bear their iniquities.

(A voice) The German reads, He is bearing their iniquities.

That is it. Behold, the Lamb of God bears. That is true. He takes sin away, and he takes it away because/he bears the sin of the world. He bears all things. How?—By the word of his power. That word you see, is in us bearing, living, acting, energetic, and it fills it. Everything is clear, open, because he is there, because he fills it, and by his knowledge shall he justify many, for he bears their iniquity. Well, then, you and I can be glad that the Lord knows all about us because of the knowledge by which he justifies us. How does he know?—Because he feels. All right, then; let him bear it. You have it all. Then you are justified, delivered, free. O, there is the comfort of it!

O, this opens up so wide a field, so many different things, I just stand in wonder! Which one shall we start out on first from this central station? Why, everything that God has for us, all truth, branches out from this. What line shall we study first? Let us look at the question of religious liberty a moment. It begins right with the individual. There is freedom. What is the bondage?—Sin. You shall know the truth, and the truth shall make you free. We are set free from what?—From sin. But think that is not all. God is with us, in us, continually bearing our infirmities. You know what Stephen said about the Jews, that "about the space of forty years suffered he their manners in the wilderness." He literally "suffered" their ways, for all their sins pressed on him. He says, "Thou hast made me to serve with thy sins, thou hast wearied me with thine iniquities. I, even I, am He that blotteth out thy transgressions for mine own sake." Isa. 43 : 24, 25.

Do you take that in? Do you see that point? Says God, Thou hast worn me out, wearied me, with thine iniquities. Why?—Because it was his life his Word, that bore it; because we piled the sin upon him, and continued to pile it upon him, and would not allow the Word to do that for which it was there all the time; viz., to take away the iniquity: God says, "I, even I, am he that blotteth our thy sin." What for?—"For mine own sake,"—in order to get rid of all this burden of sin that is piled upon him,—that is what he does it for, because he is weary of it. He says, I will do all that *for mine own sake*, that I may be clear from it. Doesn't that give us a firmer hold, stronger ground for confidence and trust and rejoicing, in the Lord?

(A voice) Yes.

Here I am; all my burden of sin is on God, on God's own life. Now he says, For mine own sake I will blot it out; it wearies me. Notwithstanding that our sins wearied the Lord all these years, he has been with us, patiently enduring it. He didn't get excited and irritable, and turn about and say, Go away; I will not endure this any longer. Didn't it stir his mind to have all that done?—Yes. But O, the infinite patience of God! He waited, waited; the long-suffering of God waited, and his long-suffering is salvation. If God hadn't been long-suffering, I could not be saved. But he waited all those long years, waited, waited, waited; and by and by his loving patience got through the thick roll of sin that had been drawn over my eyes, and I consented to let him have his own way. Now can any man who knows the Lord, and how God bears with him,—can he go about trying to regulate others, and set them right?—He cannot; it is impossible.

(A voice), He is the only man that won't do that.

Certainly. No matter how much a man may claim to believe in religious liberty, if he doesn't know the freedom that God alone gives, the time will come when he will seek to compel others. This knowledge of God will make us wonderfully charitable with one another. What a renovation it would make in our church work, if every one knew this! What forbearance and kindness, forbearing one another in love, and dealing tenderly with those who are out of the way. That would make a vast difference in the church, make a vast difference in our dealing with those who do not know the Lord and those who in their ignorance are fighting against the Lord. It would make a vast difference in our talking about being persecuted, and others opposing us. We have no opponents. Those who we sometimes think are opposing us are opposing the Lord; opposing the truth. We only need to be patient, and trust. I remember reading a Jewish legend,—it comes from the Talmud, I think,—very striking, even if it be not true, and I do not know any reason why it may not be true, except that it does not seem to be in keeping with the character of Abraham. An old man came to Abraham's tent one night asking for lodging, and Abraham hospitably took him in; but when something to eat was set before him, he began without recognition of any supreme being. Abraham asked him why he did not give thanks to God. He said he did not recognize God. He worshiped the fire, and did not see any other being to worship; so Abraham, in his zeal for God, thrust him out of the tent. By and by a storm arose, and the Lord came called, "Abraham, where is that old man I sent to you for shelter?"—"O, he worshippeth not thee, and I cast him out." And the Lord said, "I have endured him for one hundred years; could not you endure him for one night?"

When I think of how much the Lord has had to endure from me, and of the wonderful patience he has had, *and has still*, O, it is so easy to have not only sympathy and patience, but love for those who are ignorant, and who are out of the way. Well, if we learn this lesson, we shall have the key of religious liberty, and everybody has got to learn it if he gets to heaven. I tell you, brethren, this religious liberty is not a side issue that some two or three may have, and they are to carry it on, and we do not know anything about it, because it is too deep for us; brethren, if you do not know anything about it, you will never get into the kingdom of heaven. It is just as deep as the salvation of God, as broad as that, as simple as that. It is the question of life, the life of the Word of God, which is living, energy, and working,—self-working,—it is righteousness. Therefore if the Word is in us, it will work out righteousness. Take the verse before us: Let us therefore hold fast our confession—in your Bibles it is "profession," but it is *confession* in the Revised Version, and that is the exact rendering—let us hold fast our confession. What is the confession?—The confession is, that Jesus is come in the flesh. Now let us hold fast the confession of our faith. What is the trouble with us?—It is that we do not hold fast to our confession. If we confess and continue to hold fast the confession,—that Jesus Christ is come in the flesh, that the Word is nigh us, even in our mouth and in our heart, the word of faith which we preach—if we shall confess with our mouth the Lord Jesus, that he is come in our flesh, and shall believe in our heart that God hath raised him from the dead—that he is a living power, we shall be saved. It is simple, is it not? Can you see how it is done? No, we cannot see how it is done, but it is true. It is the mystery of the seed planted, which grows, although you cannot see the life in it. You cannot see any indications of life in it, but it is there. You cannot see how it does grow, when it grows; but it springs up, we know not how. That is the mystery of the Word,—the seed in us.

Now when we confess, and then let the Word have free course to be glorified, it does the work; it works us; it manifests itself in good works in our lives. "Not by works done in righteousness which we did ourselves [as we read in the third chapter of Titus], but according to his mercy he saves us, by the washing of regeneration and renewing of the Holy Ghost; which he shed on us abundantly through Jesus Christ our Saviour. That being justified by grace, we should be made heirs according to the hope of eternal life. This is a faithful saying, and these things I will that thou affirm constantly, that they which believe in God may be careful,"—to do good works?—No; but "that we which believe in God might be careful to keep good works." These things are profitable. It is not that we should be careful to do good works, but to keep the good works which God gives us, and let the good works work. That is justification by faith; and it is the message itself; it is everything. Now, why will you limit it? How many works will it do? "The man of God may be thoroughly furnished unto all good works"—except the works of the Conference? Will it do these good works in the man too? It is ample for all good works. But have not you all said that the Word of God is good to a certain extent; but then God leaves it to us to work it out? That is a mistake. The Word is profitable for doctrine, for reproof, for correction, for instruction in righteousness, that the man of God may be perfect, thoroughly furnished unto all good works; and that is the Word, the inspired Word, the Word breathed in. Christ breathed on his disciples, and said, Receive ye the Holy Ghost; and so he breathes into us the living Word, and we receive it, and believe that it is the living Word, and this new, energetic, and living way, we live by faith just as the body lives by breathing.

I will tell you the trouble; when we start out on life of this kind, it means the giving of one's self to the Word; it means thinking upon the Word, letting the Word itself dominate our thoughts. A good deal easier thing than that is to get together an hour or two, or several hours, and plan how we shall do, and resolve to work those plans, and then we do not have to think any more. It is a good deal easier to think a little once in a while than it is to think all the time, and when the Word abides in us, it will keep us thinking and working,—the Word is active energy; it works.

Now there is another line; this works righteousness. It means righteousness then, to us, the law of God working in us, working out its own righteousness in us. And this pertains to temporal as well as eternal things; for godliness is profitable unto all things, having promise not only of the life which now is, but of that which is to come.

God himself is personally present in all his works. He himself is the energy that is manifest in all creation. God himself is force, the force that is manifest in all matter. When we went to school and studied heathen philosophy, we learned that matter itself possessed certain properties, did we not?—that force was inherent in matter. That is to say, we learned that matter was God, and God was out of the question. But God himself is force; he is power,—and Jesus Christ is the wisdom of God, and the power of God. Now suppose we recognize the fact that we all live through the life of God, and only by the life of God. In the beginning everything manifested the perfection of God's life. In the creation, the new creation, everything was good and perfect. God beheld all things, and they were very good. Christ, who descended into the grave, has also ascended, that he might fill all things. That is, to make all things as they were in the beginning; everything to be full of his life. Is everything full of God's life now?—O, no; men are not. Men have held down the truth—Christ—in unrighteousness. But by recognizing, and yielding to the Spirit, we may be filled with all the perfection of God. God designs to fill us, even in our mortal bodies. Then, when the time comes, the process will be carried a step further, and the bodies be made immortal, and free from corruption. There is but one life, God's life, and therefore but one law, and that law is the law of life, the law of the Spirit of life, the law of God's life. It is not a thing he has arbitrarily laid down, but it is simply the result of God's existence.

We talk about natural and moral law. What is the difference? Take, for instance, the plants that grow according to certain laws. We can observe that certain kinds of plants, when uninterfered with, always grow in a certain way, and other plants always conform to a certain law, and we say, These plants grow according to a law! But what law?—The law is God's life in them, God's life that chooses for them the place and the thing which is best for them; that which will tend to their most perfect development after their kind. His life in them is called natural law, because nothing more is expected of them than simply to grow. They have not the order of intelligence and accountability that man has. Now man is a higher order of plant. He is a plant of the highest order, a movable plant, which God designed for the very highest position in the universe. The life of God in him, if unhindered and not interfered with, will bring him up to the perfection which God designed for him; he is a moral being,—that is, he has to do with right and wrong, and therefore the life in him works morality, and so it is called the moral law. But what is the difference? It is one law in all, bringing every created thing, from the lowest vegetable up to man, to the perfection which God has planned for it after its kind; bringing the grass to perfection as grass, and bringing the vine,—a higher order of plant with a higher office to serve,—to perfection as a vine; and the oak-tree, still more powerful, to perfection as an oak-tree; and the man to perfection as a man; but one life in it all, one law through it all. But then we do not see the fullness of God's life manifested in man, because he represses it; therefore, for man's sake and on man's account, we do not see the fullness of life in the rest of creation.

The curse of God is upon the earth, because of man's sin. God said, "Because thou hast done this, when thou tillest the earth, it shall not yield its strength to thee." And because it does not yield its strength, what does it bring forth?—Thorns and thistles. These are not a new creation, not something especially created sin order to be a curse. God did not create sin in order to curse man, but sin is a curse because it represses the life of God, which seeks unhindered circulation. The curse is a repression of it, a perversion of it, a holding of it down. So the curse that came on the earth was simply man's dominion sympathizing with him. Man had fallen, and the same fall and the same curse passed over onto the earth, and so it does not yield its strength. The fullness of God's life is not manifest in it. It is in sympathy with man, and because the fullness of God's life is not manifested, instead of bringing forth a perfect plant, it brings forth a plant with thorns on it. Where there should be fruit or flower, the imperfect, degenerate plant brings forth a thorn. How many of you have actually seen this thing, so that you can illustrate it? How many have seen a plum-tree in a neglected garden, uncultivated and uncared for, that was all covered with thorns? If that tree had been cultivated and cared for, it would not have been covered with thorns, but would have had fruit on it. It is simply degeneration. It does not yield its strength any more.

Because of the curse, we do not see anything in its perfection, yet in the inanimate creation, that is, in plants, we find the life of God most perfectly manifested. In the beginning God said, "Behold, I have given you every herb bearing seed...and every tree, in the which is the fruit of a tree yielding seed; to you it shall be for meat." We take the corn and the wheat, and there is life in them. We eat them, and the life that is in them comes into us and becomes our lives. We are built up by the life of God that is in them. The life that was in that growing plant is stored up now in the seed, and when we take it and assimilate it, all the mighty power that was manifested in bringing the seed out of the ground and perfecting it, becomes ours, and may be manifested in us; and if we will only be just as subservient, just as pliable, just as passive in the hands of God as the plant is, then we shall have the perfection of God's life wrought out in us, even in our poor, mortal bodies. On account of the original sin, the curse is now upon the earth, so that some things have the life of God less fully than others. There is a difference even in plants. Some are now poisonous, whereas in the beginning there was nothing that would cause death. Now for the practical application of this matter,—for the consideration of the relation which the food we eat sustains to our religious life. But the hour has expired, and we must take this up next time.

(Compiler's Note: There apparently was no *next time*. There are no more studies recorded under the title, *Studies in Hebrews*.)

We invite you to view the complete
selection of titles we publish at:

www.TEACHServices.com

or write or email us your praises,
reactions, or thoughts about this
or any other book we publish at:

TEACH Services, Inc.
P.O. Box 954
Ringgold, GA 30736

info@TEACHServices.com

Finally, if you are interested in seeing
your own book in print, please contact us at

publishing@teachservices.com.

We would be happy to review your manuscript for free.

www.ingramcontent.com/pod-product-compliance
Lightning Source LLC
Chambersburg PA
CBHW070540170426
43200CB00011B/2489